The
Minister's Manual

The
Minister's Manual

Evangel
Publishing House
Nappanee, Indiana

The Minister's Manual. Copyright © 1991 by Evangel Publishing House, 2000 Evangel Way, P.O. Box 189, Nappanee, Indiana 46550. All rights reserved.

All scriptural quotations are from *The Holy Bible, New International Version.* Copyright © 1973, 1978, 1984 International Bible Society. Used by permission of Zondervan Bible Publishers.

ISBN-10: 0-916035-47-6
ISBN-13: 978-0-916035-47-1

PHOTOTYPESET ◆ FOR QUALITY

Printed in the United States of America

9 8 7 6 5 4

Contents

Preface

The most recent revision of *The Minister's Manual* until now is dated 1970. In twenty years many things change in language and the way we do things; this is true of the church so that a review of handbooks and manuals is necessary. Some changes have been made in organizational structure. The widespread preference of the New International Version of the Bible among us over the King James Version warrants adjustment in the minister's printed resources (thus, let it be noted that most biblical quotations in this manual are from the NIV). A less formal approach in many quarters calls for different forms and language in the rituals of a people.

Late in the 1970s the Board of Administration appointed a committee to work on a revision. The committee developed principles for the revision and adopted a general outline. A writer from the committee, Owen H. Alderfer, was appointed and work was begun. An editorial committee reviewed the work at various stages. The general church officers did a final pre-publication review.

This manual has been carefully prepared and subjected to the scrutiny of pastors and church leaders in the hope that the needs of our church will be accountably met. We commend it to you in hope that it may be a help in performing faithful and effective service in the worship of God.

The final paragraph of the preface of the previous edition applies well to this new edition:

"Ritual does not assure nor its absences guarantee reality in worship. The principle stated by Jesus to the Samaritan woman is valid today, 'God is a Spirit, and they that worship him must worship him in spirit and in truth.' It should be the constant concern of the minister that the congregation finds reality in the public worship services of the church. It is the hope of those responsible for the preparation of this manual that it will aid in providing services of worship that are meaningful to the worshipper and acceptable to God."

Acknowledgements

From the 1970 edition

The history of ritual and orders of public worship in the Christian Church reaches back to New Testament times. A manual, although compiled to meet the needs of a segment of the Universal Church and oriented to the present age, is the richer when, with that which is current and distinctive, are included forms and settings which have stood the test of time.

The editors of *A Manual for Ministers* have included in this manual certain forms and phrases which have come to us from the Church of the past. We believe that the manual will be the more useful and its ministry the richer because these have been included. The editors have also been alert to forms and orders of service used by other evangelical churches. A number of these forms seemed appropriate and were included, usually with adaptations and settings distinctive to this manual.

We are greatly indebted to these who have so willingly granted permission to use the materials which they control. We wish to express our indebtedness and appreciation to the following for the use of copyrighted material in the preparation of this manual:

The Standard Publishing Company for use of the following material from the *Christian Minister's Manual, 1937:* the ritual of dedication in the Dedication of a Baptistry (with adaptations), page 132; the act of dedication in the Dedication of a Church Building, pages 125 and 126; and the act of dedication in the service of Dedication of an Organ (with adaptations), pages 134 and 135.

The Board of Christian Education of the Presbyterian Church U.S.A. for use from *The Book of Common Worship, 1933*, the ritual [adapted] for the installation of members of the ministry team, pages 114 and 115.

The United Free Church of Scotland for use from *The Book of Common Order, 1928*, the [second] committal prayer [adapted] on page 94.

The Fleming H. Revell Company for use from *Hymns for the Living Age* the prayer for Good Friday [altered] found on pages 174 and 175.

The editors found the *Minister's Service Book, 1937*, edited by James D. Morrison and published by Harper and Brothers, a valuable source of prayers. We wish to express to Harper and Brothers our appreciation for permission to use the following: the prayer by Samuel McComb on page 85; the third invocation on page 165; the offertory prayer by Arthur Cleaves on page 170; a prayer for the New Year by James D. Morrison on page 174, and a prayer by the same author for Easter on page 175 (altered); the Mother's Day prayer by D. W. Conrad on page 176 (altered).

We are also indebted to Harper and Brothers for permission to use from the *Minister's Service Book* a major portion of the ritual for the installation of Sunday School Teachers and Officials.

Having a heritage which has much in common with that of the Evangelical United Brethren denomination resulted in our finding appropriate a number of the rituals used by that denomination. We are, therefore, much indebted to The Otterbein Press for permission to use the following materials taken from *The Book of Ritual, 1955:* the ritual of dedication used at the service of Dedication of an Educational Building (with adaptations) as found on pages 132 and 133; the service of Dedication of a Home (with adaptations); the ritual of dedication in the Dedication of a Parsonage; the questions and answers (with adaptations) related to the Consecration of the Bishops; the declaration by the bishop and the charge to the missionaries [altered] on page 109; the service of Mortgage or Note Burning (altered) as found on pages 147 and 148.

Additional acknowledgements
for the 1991 edition

From *Minister's Service Manual,* published in 1958 by Baker Book House, Grand Rapids, Michigan, the poem on pages 184 and 185 by Clinton Lockhart.

From *The Pastor's Manual,* edited by James Randolph Hobbs and published in 1962 by Broadman Press, Nashville, Tennessee, the poems of consolation on pages 180 to 183 by Henry Drummond, John L. McCreery, and Horatius Bonar.

From *The Pastor's Manual* of the Church of the Brethren, copyright 1978, the alternate service of child dedication, pages 48 and 49. From the Church of the Brethren Annual Conference Statement 1983, "The Office of Deacon," the service of consecration of a deacon (with adaptations), pages 105 to 107.

From *Masterpieces of Religious Verse,* edited by James Dalton Morrison and published in 1948 by Harper and Brothers, New York, the poems of consolation on pages 180 to 185 by John Donne, Alexander Pope, Henry Wadsworth Longfellow, James Montgomery, and Frederick L. Hosmer.

From *The Worshipbook: Services and Hymns.* Copyright © 1970, 1972, The Westminster Press, the prayer on page 86, the prayer on page 90, and the four prayers and the benediction on pages 92 and 93. Used by permission of Westminister/John Knox Press.

The hymn text, "Children of the Heavenly Father," pages 186-187, copyright © Board of Publication, Lutheran Church in America. Reprinted by permission of Augsburg Fortress.

A diligent effort has been made to determine the source of materials used in this manual and to obtain permission in those cases where copyrights are involved. In case there has been failure to obtain permission, we regret this oversight and welcome this matter being called to our attention.

Use of This Book

Purpose of this Manual

The purpose of this manual is the same as that of the previous edition: "to aid the minister in planning the regular worship services with propriety and the occasional service with confidence" (1970 edition). The rituals of a body are a reflection of the doctrines and beliefs as expressed in the worship services, ordinances, and ceremonies of the Christian Church. The rituals included in this manual are consistent with the beliefs of the evangelical church. Rigid conformity in the use of these exercises is not required nor expected; however, deviation from the form presented should be done with care so that what is done is consistent with the denomination's official positions as found in the *Manual of Doctrine and Government.*

Orientation to the Manual

This *Minister's Manual* is for people of a free church tradition. The orders of worship are not to be seen as binding upon us; rather, they are presented as models around which to develop functional services of balance, beauty, and direction. Religious services do have form; they should be developed with thought and clarity in the interest of leading people into the presence of God.

The inclusion of a large section on "Aids for Use in Worship and Other Services of the Church" may suggest formalism. The concern, however, is to encourage thoughtful preparation for worship and prayer. The worship aids are a ready reference for use in preparing the worship service. The prayers are for the inspiration and guidance of the minister in leading the people before God. Generally these will not be read verbatim, for there is no substitute for free and spontaneous prayer. A study of the prayers included here will enrich the public prayers of the minister and add to them beauty and meaning.

Use the manual as a tool in the work of ministry. It is designed to be your servant in the work, but never to be your master.

Plan of the Manual

This *Minister's Manual* is comprised of seven sections. The first section begins with some personal words to the minister about the meaning and significance of ministry. Section II moves to the heart of the minister's public service, preparation for worship. This section includes orders of the basic worship service of the week and refers to a variety of aids found in Section VII. The materials presented here are suggestive rather than exhaustive; they should be helpful to the pastor as "starters."

Sections III, IV, and V are patterns for rituals to guide the pastor in planning for special occasions and events that are a part of the ministry and program of the church. Section III is given to the Christian ordinances, baptism and communion. Section IV focuses on ministry to persons in the special moments of the human journey from birth to death. The "Ministry at the Time of Death" portion includes many scriptural passages appropriate for use in such times. The minister will also want to be aware of the inclusion of poems and hymns of consolation in the latter part of Section VII for ministry in times of grief and preparation for funeral occasions.

Section V covers a broad spectrum of special church occasions. Included are rites for ordination, services of consecration of persons to various ministries, services of installation to various offices and ministries, services of dedication of church facilities and homes, and services associated with the physical and fiscal matters of the church. The minister may use verbatim the model services in Sections III, IV, and V, or may make appropriate additions and changes to enhance the services.

Section VI calls attention to the use of the Christian calendar—special times and seasons to which the minister may give attention in planning work, worship services, and special programs.

Section VII, mentioned above, is a resource section for the minister in developing worship services and in ministry at the time of death. Also included are two historic creeds of the Church, the Apostles Creed and the Nicene Creed. Following this are five divisions of helps for the preparation of the principal worship services of the church, arranged in the usual order of the worship service: calls to worship, invocations, offertory sentences and prayers, the pastoral prayer (including prayers for special days and seasons), and benedictions. These helps are largely oriented to Scripture for the use of Bible-believing people. The section concludes with a presentation of Easter dates through 2013.

In using this manual, some reference back and forth within the book will be necessary. This is especially the case in dealing with Section VII, Aids and Reference. In developing the worship service, the minister may want to refer repeatedly to this section in shaping the relevant parts. Notation of the date of use should be made to ensure that the minister does not unwittingly repeat the use of respective elements from Sunday to Sunday. Cross referencing with Section VII may also be necessary in preparing for ministry at the time of death.

As the minister becomes acquainted with this manual, may it become a ready help and a useful tool in Christian ministry.

Section I
The Minister

The Minister

This is a handbook for ministers; therefore, in beginning it is appropriate to address some words to the minister as person.

No calling is higher and no vocation more demanding than that of the Christian minister. Paul states, "It was he [God] who gave some to be apostles, some to be prophets, some to be evangelists, and some to be pastors and teachers" (Ephesians 4:11). The pastor is God's gift to the church for the equipping of the people in the work of ministry.

The minister comes to the task with a sense of calling, accompanied by appropriate equipment: a thriving relationship to Jesus Christ as Savior and Lord, mastery of the Word, understanding of Christian doctrine, love for the church as the body of Christ, compassion for people, and knowledge of the easiest routes to the human heart.

Brilliance, eloquence, and physical attractiveness are not necessary requirements for the minister; devotion, faithfulness, and compassion are. Throughout history, and in wondrous ways, God has used persons who are fully available to him; he does so still. All God asks is that the minister give full measure of energy and dedication in the work at hand. This devotion must be balanced among obligations to family and care of one's own physical needs, for the minister is a model to others in human relationships and in the stewardship of life.

The minister should reflect sensitivity and care in relationship to and within a congregation. In a new pastorate it generally is wise to begin with current custom and practices. Acceptance of local folkways and congregational structures and style will avoid unnecessary confrontation. Desired changes can be made in due time. Learn to know the people of the parish, those within the church first, and in the broader community later. Remember there is no substitute for personal relationships. Learn to know family members by name and know the particular needs, burdens and interests of each. Jesus declared, "Even the Son of Man did not come to be served, but to serve, and to give his life as a ransom for many" (Mark 10:45). The minister follows the example of the Master.

The faithful pastor sees to it that people are ministered to in their times of need: sickness, accident, trial, bereavement. Hospital and sickroom visits demand a quiet confidence and the tact of sensitivity. In times of sorrow the pastor shares the grief of the bereft, expresses sympathy, and reaches out to the sorrowing with understanding love. With the confessing sinner, the pastor is firm and supportive, loving the sinner but dealing responsibly with sin.

One of the highest challenges for the minister is in bringing the people into the presence of God in worship. The worship experience is approached with due thought and preparation as to its components and the words themselves. Prayer reflects thought and reverence. Scripture is read with clarity and force. The Word is preached clearly with the needs of the people in view.

The above comments primarily address "the minister as pastor"; that is, the concepts reflect situations in which one person leads in ministry for the broad range of needs for a congregation of 150 or less. In the congregation of 200 and more with staff assigned to various areas and a senior minister who is "manager," the work of ministry becomes complex with persons having various roles. Still, the spirit of ministry described has relevance as it is applied to the several persons involved in ministry in the areas where they are called to serve.

18

Section II
Christian Worship

Christian Worship

Preparation for Worship

Worship does not "just happen." The persons involved in leadership must be prepared in heart and mind to lead the people to God. The component parts must be thoughtfully readied so as to meld together and to blend into an holistic experience that brings the worshiper into the presence of God. Scripture is our model here. The Old Testament includes worship manuals for the people of God—these were the worship aids for the New Testament church which was taught to "worship the Father in spirit and in truth."

The minister and others who lead in public worship must prepare in spirit as well as in the forms that are a part of the worship. Such preparation takes place both in the study and in the place of prayer. The Bible plays a central role in worship; it is word from the Lord, and as such it is a crucial part of the dialogue which constitutes worship. Appropriate passages should be selected for devotion, instruction, profession of faith, adoration, etc. Giving thought in advance to the prayers that will be offered is appropriate preparation. Extemporaneous prayer can be complemented by noting the topics that need to be covered in a given service. Though our Lord Jesus Christ did not instruct us in how to preach, he did teach us how to pray. We do well to dignify the prayer times with aptly chosen language and topics suitable for the occasion.

The order of worship needs to be thoroughly prepared so that the service may proceed without awkwardness and struggle that calls attention negatively to any component part itself. These elements must be blended together with taste and ease so as to construct a beautiful whole. Worship, according to Scripture, is to be offered "in the beauty of holiness." Both dimensions, Scripture indicates, are important to God.

Above all, "God is spirit, and his worshipers must worship in spirit and in truth" (John 4:24). Those who conduct worship must lead the worshipers to God from their own sense of the presence and glory of God. Let preparation for worship begin well in advance of any given service. Let it continue in the immediate time of the service as the persons responsible lead the participants in prayer for the experience at hand. May it be expressed in the living of life in the days that follow.

A Prayer of Preparation for Worship

Lord God, our Father,

Again we have come to the time of worship. Without your Word we have nothing to say; without your own self we have nothing to give; without your power we cannot proceed. Fill us with your Holy Spirit that the Word may come alive through us, your presence may be evident and real, and each one who participates in worship today may be changed into your image by the power of the Holy Spirit. Our prayer is in Jesus' name. Amen.

The Church at Worship

In a basic sense the Christian's expression of worship depends upon God's revelation to us through Jesus Christ. We can approach God because he has come to us; we love God because he has first loved us. Since God has revealed himself to be worthy of complete trust and gratitude, we naturally wish to respond to him through worship. In the act of worship Christians remember God's crucial and significant acts, the life and sacrifice of Christ Jesus, and the Holy Spirit's activity in the church today. Our response can be none other than

> Holy, holy, holy is the Lord Almighty;
> the whole earth is full of his glory. (Isaiah 6:3)

The Scriptures present a wealth of information regarding the desirability and general nature of worship. The Psalmist invites the Hebrews to

> Glorify the Lord with me;
> let us exalt his name together. (Psalm 34:3)

Also we learn that in the act of worship we are assured that

> Blessed are those who dwell in your house;
> they are ever praising you. (Psalm 84:4)

In many Psalms the worshiper is encouraged to sing and rejoice:
At his tabernacle will I sacrifice with shouts of joy;
I will sing and make music to the Lord. (Psalm 27:6)

One can trace the roots of Christian worship directly back to the practices which took place in the Jewish synagogue. Indeed, synagogue worship included at least three principal ingredients commonly found in all forms of Christian worship today, namely, the reading of Scripture, preaching, and singing.

Within the book of Acts we discover various allusions to the practice of worship in the early church: "They devoted themselves to the apostles' teaching and to the fellowship, to the breaking of bread and to prayer" (Acts 2:42). In Acts 5:42 we read, "Day after day, in the temple courts and from house to house, they never stopped teaching and proclaiming the good news that Jesus is the Christ." In the early church, worship seems often to be associated with a common meal among believers. Thus, the account of Eutychus and his accident begins with the words, "On the first day of the week we came together to break bread" (Acts 20:7).

The New Testament account, however, is vague as it deals with an actual order of worship. We may conclude that the issue of a designated order was never one that sparked controversy, and therefore the writers saw little reason to discuss it. In his instructions to the Corinthian church, Paul suggests that believers share in "a hymn, or a word of instruction, a revelation, a tongue or an interpretation" (1 Corinthians 14:26). However, he concludes with the dictum, "But everything should be done in a fitting and orderly way" (1 Corinthians 14:40). Nevertheless, we are left with little additional information concerning this "orderly way."

The earliest description of corporate worship among Christians comes down to us in the writing of Justin Martyr (*First Apology* addressed to the Roman emperor, about 150 A. D.). Since this account provides us with information relatively close to the time of Christ and his apostles, it is helpful to observe the order of events:

    (1) Reading of Scripture from both Old and New Testaments

    (2) Delivery of the sermon based upon the previous Scriptures

    (3) Offering of prayers apparently done in silence after the bidding of the leader

(4) The kiss of peace

(5) Giving of offerings presumably by believers actually carrying provisions (bread and wine) to the front of the room

(6) Delivery of the eucharistic prayer; that is, relating the words and acts of Jesus on the occasion of the Last Supper

(7) Receiving of communion by the assembled believers

Orders of Worship

The following "Order of Worship" attempts to incorporate in logical sequence: preparation for worship, praise and adoration, prayer, exposition of God's Word, Scripture reading, and music. The tradition of the Brethren in Christ has never called for a rigid adherence to any set pattern of worship. This "Order of Worship," then, should be viewed as a model or guide, and not one that must be adhered to strictly.

Prelude (usually organ, if available)
Pastoral Greeting
Introit (choir or soloist)
Call to Worship
Invocation

Hymn
Responsive Reading
Pastoral Prayer
Music Ministry

Hymn
The Church in Community (greeting of one another)
Offertory Sentence
Offering (with music by instrumentalist or choir)
Offertory Response (sung by the congregation)

Reading of the Scripture Lesson
Sermon or Message
Hymn

Benediction and/or Invitation
Postlude

Many congregations would be at home with a less formal order of worship. The following is offered as a model for such congregations:

Announcements
Call to Worship and Invocation
Hymn(s)
Scripture Lesson
Praise and Prayer (a sharing and informal time)
Pastoral Prayer
Hymn
Offering and Offertory
Music Ministry (choir or special group)
Sermon
Benediction and/or Invitation

Aids for Worship

Practical Suggestions
The pastor may wish to consider the following suggestions which will assist in creating a more effective worship service:

(1) *Involve the congregation*—The pastor should be alert to opportunities which will involve the congregation directly in the worship service. Of course, congregational singing is an important part of the morning worship service. Other areas which offer meaningful opportunities for participation are the Call to Worship, the Responsive Reading, and the Offertory Sentence. On occasion it is well also to include corporate recitation of the Ten Commandments, the Lord's Prayer, and the Apostles' Creed. Personal testimony, expressions of thanksgiving, and statements of prayer requests may be a meaningful aspect of congregational involvement in some congregations.

(2) *Unify the Service*—The pastor can create greater unity in the worship service through the application of a single theme or topic. Naturally, such a theme generally grows out of the sermon topic or Scripture lesson. Through careful selection of texts, such components as hymns, responsive reading, and the music ministry can contribute to the central theme. Of course, organizing a unified service will require careful planning several weeks in advance of the worship service.

Aids for Planning and Conducting Worship Services

Worship manuals and some hymnbooks provide orders of worship. The minister is encouraged to use such materials as models and to develop personal sensitivity and skills in preparing orders of worship that have meaning for the given setting of worship.

Section VII of this handbook is a collection of aids for use in worship and other services of the church. From these materials the worship leader may select appropriate materials to enrich and enhance the worship service. Aids of particular value to worship services include:

Calls to Worship	Pages 156-164
Invocations	Pages 165-167
Offertory Sentences	Pages 168-170
Benedictions	Pages 178-179

Other Services

Gatherings of the congregation for services other than Sunday morning have been a part of the evangelical Christian scene in North America for a century and more. Services with a clear purpose on Sunday evening and at midweek can strengthen and extend the church. Therefore, comment relative to these services is in order in a manual such as this.

Sunday Evening Service

The pastor, working with the resources of the congregation, will want to discern the needs of the church and design Sunday evening services and activities in accordance with the needs that are evident. Some congregations have found informal home groups led by undershepherds a meaningful alternative. Some use Sunday evening as a time for addressing special need areas for the congregation such as family, witnessing, Bible content, Christian social issues, and the like. Former things have passed away and the church is called to new approaches in its use of Sunday evening.

Midweek Service

The congregation will want to accept the challenge to provide meaningful activities that will minister effectively. Some churches find midweek the ideal time for children's clubs and activities to be in session. Some find this a time for Christian service and ministries programs, so that task forces are functioning in a variety of areas such as evangelism, music, nurture, and the like. Other churches make this a training night for church school teachers and other workers in the church school programs. Clearly, the midweek service dare not mimic Sunday morning or Sunday evening; it will have to meet felt needs if there is hope for anyone to attend.

Section III
The Christian Ordinances

Baptism

Background: Believers Baptism

The Brethren in Christ have a heritage in Anabaptism in which the common custom of infant baptism was rejected as being no baptism at all. In that movement, people were burned at the stake or drowned because they insisted that baptism is a decisive act of a responsible believer and they chose to be baptized as adults whatever the cost. We are part of a church in which for more than two hundred years all those people who became members of the church were baptized as believers. Given this history, baptism is seen as a witness to faith; therefore, it is good for the members of a church and others who are part of that church—and perhaps considering baptism or membership—to hear the testimonies of those who are being baptized because of their faith in Jesus Christ and obedience to his command.

Preparation and Instruction

Instruction prior to baptism is necessary both for understanding of the theological implications of the rite and for preparation of the candidate to experience the act itself. Upon satisfactory completion of instruction, the minister presents the names of applicants for baptism to the church board for consideration and consent for administering of the rite. The pastor is responsible for the spiritual and theological preparation of candidates; the deacons or other duly appointed persons are responsible for the physical arrangements necessary for baptism. Brethren in Christ baptism is by trine immersion, baptizing people three times forward and completely under the water.

In the early church, baptism was the culmination rite in a process of entrance into the church. It signified both conversion and the resulting covenant with the Christian community. Certainly then, baptism follows conversion, and it is for people who are entering into covenant with the church. Baptism is a function of the worshiping community.

Jesus clearly commands baptism in Matthew 28. Paul's description of baptism in Romans 6 is best understood as the action of an adult believer. For those who are uncomfortable being what they call "rebaptized," we have a gentle teaching responsibility. Part of our defense is given above, part will be an interpretation of various relevant passages of Scripture; e.g., Matthew 28:18-19; Romans 6:3ff; 1 Peter 3:21; Colossians 2:12, 3:1-3. Another area of concern will be in asking questions about what baptism in the New Testament symbolizes. It is not the dedication-like event when parents bring their infant children to the church; nor is there any clear connection in the New Testament between circumcision (which was performed only on males) and baptism.

The Rite of Water Baptism

The rite of baptism often follows the sermon in a worship service of the congregation. Local practice may govern the time and situation of the performance of the rite.

Singing a hymn is appropriate in conjunction with the rite of baptism. This may be followed by a Scripture reading. Appropriate passages include:

The Baptism of Jesus	Matthew 3:13-17
The Great Commission	Matthew 28:19-20
The Day of Pentecost	Acts 2:37-47
Philip Baptizes the Eunuch	Acts 8:26-39
Baptism of Lydia	Acts 16:14-15
Conversion and Baptism of the Philippian Jailer	Acts 16:25-34
The Meaning of Baptism	Romans 6:1-11

One or more of these Scriptures may be read before the minister enters the water. The minister upon entering the water may say the following or address the applicants and the congregation as follows:

Obeying the command of our Lord Jesus, and confident of his presence with us, we have come to baptize those who have heard and responded to his call.

In Jesus Christ, God has promised to forgive our sins, and has joined us together in the family of faith which is his church.

He has delivered us from darkness and transferred us to the kingdom of his beloved Son. In Jesus Christ, God has promised to be our Father, and to receive us as brothers and sisters in Christ.

Know that the promises of God are for you. By baptism, God's sign is placed on you to show that you belong to him. Sharing Christ's reconciling work, you will also share his victory; that, dying with Christ to sin, you will be raised with him to new life.

At the indication of the minister, the applicants individually enter the water. The minister says:

My brother/sister: In coming to baptism, you declare your faith in Jesus Christ and announce that you want to be his obedient disciple.

_____(Name)_____, have you received Jesus Christ as your Savior?

Answer: Yes.

Do you believe that he has forgiven your sins?

Answer: Yes.

(The applicant may now give a personal testimony of faith in Christ.)

The minister has the applicant kneel and administers the rite by immersing the applicant three times forward, saying the following words:

Because of your confession of faith and in obedience to the command of him who is the head of the church, I baptize you into the death of Christ and to newness of life through the power of his resurrection, in the name of the Father (*first immersion*), and of the Son (*second immersion*), and of the Holy Spirit (*third immersion*). Amen.

A brief personalized prayer is appropriate after each applicant has been baptized or, if desired, upon the conclusion of the administration of the rite to all the applicants.

(continued on next page)

The service may conclude with a hymn and benediction, the benediction being in the words of the minister, or as follows:

To him who is able to keep you from falling and to present you before his glorious presence without fault and with great joy—to the only God our Savior be glory, majesty, power and authority, through Jesus Christ our Lord, before all ages, now and forevermore! Amen.

Congregations with an Anabaptist concept of the church understand Scripture to teach baptism as subsequent to conversion. Baptism is also an act of identification with a visible body of believers. When a person previously converted seeks membership but has not had believers baptism, the following shall be used. At the indication of the minister, the applicants individually enter the water. The minister says:

My brother/sister: In coming to baptism, you affirm your faith in Christ and your desire to be an obedient disciple. *The minister has the applicant kneel.* _____(Name)_____: you have evidenced your faith in Christ and your faithfulness to his teachings. As an expression of your obedience, I baptize you in the name of the Father (*first immersion*), and of the Son (*second immersion*), and of the Holy Spirit (*third immersion*). Amen.

Communion
and the Washing of the Saints' Feet

The plans for services and worship orders provided here are designed to give guidance to congregations in planning and arranging services that meet the needs of local bodies over a period of time. The first order of worship is for a communion service. The second is for a feetwashing service. A service combining feetwashing and the Lord's Supper is third, followed by instructions for a Love Feast Service.

A Service of the Lord's Supper

General
The Lord's Supper, or communion, is a time of worship for the people who have entered into the body of Christ, the church. Here believers approach the Table of the Lord to celebrate their union with Christ and with one another.

The service is one of thanksgiving (Eucharist) for what God has provided for us through the sacrifice of his Son, Jesus, the Christ. It brings to mind the physical suffering and death of Jesus; it points to the expected return of Jesus for his Bride, the Church. Inasmuch as it points to Jesus' death, it is solemn; inasmuch as it points to our future hope, it is a joyous celebration.

We are also reminded of the unity and equality of believers as we gather for communion. We are equal in that we are each made welcome through faith in the atonement of Jesus; we are in one body which is the temple of God, the dwelling place of God's Spirit.

We need to prepare for communion through prayer, self-examination, confession and renewal of commitment.

35

Scriptures

The following Scriptures are suggested both for public reading and for sermon texts:

Psalm 22:1-31	1 Corinthians 3:16-17
Isaiah 53:1-12	1 Corinthians 11:17-34
Matthew 26:1-13; 14-15; 16-30	Ephesians 4:1-6
Mark 14:1-9; 10-11; 12-26	Philippians 2:5-11
Luke 22:1-6; 7-23	Hebrews 8:1-13
John 6:48-58	Hebrews 10:1-25
John 13:1-17	1 John 3:11-24
John 19:1-37	

An Order of Service

The suggested outline for the principal worship service (see "The Church at Worship," p. 24) will be adapted to incorporate the communion service. The Lord's Supper may be served before the sermon or as the culmination of worship following the sermon.

Further adaptations may be made for serving the Lord's Supper at other times (evening, Passion Week, etc.). A service for those shut-in would be brief and fitted to the condition of the participant (a hymn, Scripture reading, prayer, and the serving of the elements, for instance).

Clearly, there is a measure of individuality and diversity in the way in which communion and associated rites are observed. The evident spontaneity and freedom of worship is to be appreciated. It is appropriate, however, that this be balanced with a measure of denominational uniformity in the more formal communion service and the rituals so that Brethren in Christ members have a sense of at-homeness in the general observances in denominational gatherings and in the several congregations of the denomination, regardless of where they are.

The Lord's Supper

Invitation (in the pastor's own words, or as follows):

We now invite you to come to this table, not because you must, but because you may. Come to testify not that you are perfect, but that you sincerely love our Lord Jesus Christ and desire to be his true disciple. Come, not because you are strong, but because you are weak; not because you have any claim on heaven's rewards, but because in your frailty you stand in constant need of heaven's mercy and help. Now that the supper of the Lord is spread before you, lift up your minds and hearts above all selfish fears and cares. Let this bread and this cup be to you the witness of the grace of our Lord Jesus Christ, the love of God, and the communion of the Holy Spirit.

(A statement should be made reminding the participants of the necessity of being in a right relationship with Christ and with brothers and sisters.)

Words of Institution for the Bread
The night when Jesus was betrayed, he took bread, blessed it, broke it, and gave it to his disciples. We follow his example. Let us pray.

Prayer of Blessing on the Bread *(in the pastor's own words)*

The Ritual
Minister: Friends, is not this bread the communion of the body of Christ?
People: This bread is the communion of the body of Christ.

Passing the Bread
Take and eat this bread, remembering that he was born to be our Savior; he was wounded for our transgressions; he was bruised for our iniquities. Feed on him in your heart and be thankful.

Words of Institution for the Cup
The night when Jesus was betrayed, he also took the cup, blessed it, and gave it to his disciples. We do likewise. Let us pray.

Prayer of Blessing on the Cup *(in the pastor's own words)*

The Ritual
Minister: Friends, is not this cup the communion of the blood of Christ?
People: This cup is the communion of the blood of Christ.

Passing the Cup
Take this cup, remembering that he said, "This is my blood of the covenant, which is poured out for many for the forgiveness of sins." Drink of it together and be thankful.

Practical Considerations

The format of the communion service will need to be suited to the number of participants and the facilities available. When served during the principal worship time, the participants will probably remain in the pews and be served there. On other occasions, the participants may gather as a whole or in groups around the communion table and be served there. It may be suitable to share the Lord's Supper around tables in a fellowship room with or without a full Love Feast meal.

Washing the Saints' Feet

Background

The washing of the saints' feet is a part of the Brethren in Christ heritage from its early Anabaptist roots, with its focus on being faithful to the teaching of John 13. In earlier times the Lord's Supper was seldom—if ever—observed apart from feetwashing. In the process of time it became convenient, necessary, and appropriate to observe the Lord's Supper apart from feetwashing, in conjunction with the worship of the congregation on a Sunday morning. Time strictures made the inclusion of the feetwashing ritual practically impossible in view of these changes.

Many congregations, as a result, observe the Lord's Supper without feetwashing two or more times a year and a combined service of feetwashing and the Lord's Supper once or twice each year. The service is conducted sometimes on Maundy Thursday as a part of Holy Week services. Other congregations observe feetwashing as a service of self-examination and preparation for the Lord's Supper. Still other congregations have found blessing in reviving the traditional Love Feast, incorporating the Agape or Fellowship Meal with the services of feetwashing and the Lord's Supper.

A Combined Service: Washing the Saints' Feet and the Lord's Supper

Approach to Worship
  Music and hymns, calling to worship, and invocation

The Rite of Feetwashing
Scripture Lesson John 13:1-17

Prayer (in the pastor's own words)

Meditation on Feetwashing
  This should deal with the deep and abiding lessons from Jesus' example of serving, avoiding moralizing and sentimentality. The force of Jesus' washing his disciples' feet is fourfold, namely: obligation (v. 14); example (v. 15); comparison (v. 16); and blessing (v. 17) [Cf. Joseph R. Shultz, *The Soul of the Symbols,* Grand Rapids, MI: William B. Eerdmans Publishing Company, 1966, pp. 76-77]. Herein we enact together a rite that recognizes our need of continual cleansing and our interaction in cleansing and caring through mutual participation.

Sharing
  Following the meditation and/or during the rite of feetwashing, time may well be given to sharing among believers—praise, purpose, confession of faith, and confession of faults and needs.

The Ritual
  The scriptural practice of the washing of the saints' feet and of the Holy Kiss (sometimes referred to as the Kiss of Peace), an accompanying rite expressing affection and affirmation, is observed under the direction of the deacons and their spouses. It is preferable that the men and the women retire to separate rooms for this observance. The minister will make such explanations and give such instructions as are appropriate and necessary. The rite is generally conducted in circle units (the number of circles depending on the number of participants) as follows: The first person ties a towel around himself/herself and places a basin before the next person in the circle. The recipient places the feet in the basin (practice varies as to whether one foot or both feet are immersed at one time) and the person washing washes and dries the feet one after the other. Then the participants stand and greet

each other with the Holy Kiss. The process is then repeated with the person just washed becoming the person washing the feet of the next person in the circle, until all have been washed. Hymns and testimonies complement this part of the service. When the ritual has been concluded, the participants assemble in the sanctuary for the next portion of the service.

A hymn focusing the thoughts of the worshipers on the loving acts of Christ and his work of redemption may be sung.

The Lord's Supper

Scripture Lesson
The Suffering Savior (select one of the following passages: Psalm 22:1-31; Isaiah 53:1-12; Matthew 26:1-30; Mark 14:1-26; Luke 22:1-23; John 19:1-37)

Meditation on the Sacrifice of Christ

Prayer (in the pastor's own words)

The Invitation
The leader calls attention to the Lord's Table as the serving person uncovers the bread and cup, and says:
Let all who trust in Christ as Savior and Lord and who are in peace with their brothers and sisters observe the ordinance of the Lord's Supper in commemoration of the death and suffering of our Lord and Savior, Jesus Christ.

Words of Institution for the Bread
From this point forward, the service for the Lord's Supper is incorporated into the combined service. (See pp. 36-37 above.)

A Love Feast Service

The Love Feast Service was traditionally a weekend service including times of eating together at a common table, a service of examination and preparation for feetwashing and the Lord's Supper. For contemporary times the service may be modified and incorporated into a full service for an evening of the week or a Sunday evening. An appropriate time would be the Lenten period in the spring or near Thanksgiving time as a Harvest Festival in the fall.

The Agape Meal or Love Feast

The meal may take one of several forms in keeping with the nature and needs of the congregation: (1) a pot-luck dinner; (2) a specially prepared traditional Love Feast meal (some research may be necessary to determine what type of meal was traditional in former years); (3) a meal symbolizing the Passover meal with bitter herbs, the bread and broth, and the meat. The meal can be a time of free fellowship and interaction, or it can be one of formal direction by the leader who calls the attention of the participants to the significance of each act in the ongoing meal.

Washing the Saints' Feet

John 13:3-5 indicates that during the meal "Jesus . . . rose from supper . . . and began to wash the disciples' feet. . . ." If facilities allow, the service can move to feetwashing immediately from the tables upon completion of the meal. With a reading of John 13:1-17 and brief comments, participants leave the table and retire to the location where feetwashing is enacted. During this period a time of singing and sharing in testimony and praise may be conducted among the people.

When all have participated in the rite of feetwashing and have returned to the tables or to the sanctuary, the service proceeds to the final act of the drama.

The Lord's Supper

If facilities allow, it is most appropriate to observe the Lord's Supper around the tables where the meal was eaten. The ritual is preceded by the reading of Scripture and appropriate comments. The partaking of the bread and the cup mark the culmination of the service. (The ritual is outlined above, pp. 36-37.)

The service concludes with appropriate statements, the singing of a hymn, and prayer.

Section IV
Ministry at Special Times

Dedication of Children

The dedication of children is a rite having biblical sanction and spiritual merit. The time of welcoming a new child into a family of the church community is a tender moment, a rite of passage laden with significance and possibilities. Although the rite is not to be regarded as having ordinance value—and we believe that baptism is given only for those who are capable of repentance and faith—biblical examples and the practice of Jesus raise it to a high level of propriety.

The pastor or a designated person should be in touch with a family at the time a child is born to inform the parents of the church's desire to support them in their responsibility of parenthood. The act of child dedication affirms for both the parents and the congregation the privilege of rearing a child in a nurturing community of faith. The meaning of the dedication act should be explained to the parents ahead of time. The pastor should explain the actual steps in the rite so that the parents will approach the moment comfortably and confidently.

The service should be conducted in the presence of the congregation with the involvement of the people. For the official record, the minister should obtain the name of the child, the place and date of birth, and the names of the parents. The information should be incorporated into the church record and an appropriate certificate prepared for presentation to the child.

The rite of child dedication should be incorporated into a worship service at an appropriate point as an act of worship. In some instances it may be incorporated with a message concerning children and family. At the call of the minister, the child will be presented by the parents before the congregation.

Child dedication is not an appropriate rite in cases where parents are not committed to Christ. In such instances, however, the pastor may choose to celebrate the birth in a worship service.

The Rite of Child Dedication

Introduction (in the pastor's own words, or as follows):

As children were welcomed by Jesus, so they are welcome as a part of this congregation. As a new member of a family in this body, they are an integral part of this church. They are recipients of its blessings and mission, and experience its fellowship and traditions. As parents bring their little ones in presentation to the Lord, we covenant as a congregation to surround the child and the family with the support of the people of God.

In this rite today, parents publicly commit themselves to provide a home in which their child/children will grow up in the nurture and admonition of the Lord and where he/she/they will learn of Christ and his ways and be encouraged to receive him as Savior and Lord. Parents are the child's primary pastor and greatest influence for good and righteousness.

The Dedication
The minister calls on the parents to come before the congregation with their child. When the family is situated, the minister may make a brief introduction of parents and child. Addressing the parents the minister says:

My friends, this is a happy and blessed occasion that brings us together. Like Mary and Hannah in the Scriptures, you have brought your child in an act of presentation and dedication to the Lord. God has blessed you with this new life. In this act of dedication you recognize the seriousness of this trust and its accompanying obligations. The Scriptures state (*use one or more of the following*):

See that you do not look down on one of these little ones. For I tell you that their angels in heaven always see the face of my Father in heaven.   (Matthew 18:10)

These commandments that I give you today are to be upon your hearts. Impress them on your children. Talk about them when you sit at home and when you walk along the road, when you lie down and when you get up. (Deuteronomy 6:6-7)

Train a child in the way he should go, and when he is old he will not turn from it.   (Proverbs 22:6)

Minister: Almighty God has been gracious to you in giving you the gift of this child. Do you now present your child before God in dedication?

Parents: We do.

Minister: Is it your purpose to bring up your child in the ways of the Lord?

Parents: It is.

Minister: Will you continue to love each other and the child God has given you so that he/she will experience the meaning of trust and grace?

Parents: We will.

Minister: Will you endeavor to provide a Christian home and atmosphere for your child? Will you teach him/her in the Christian faith and way, surround him/her with Christian influences through the church and other relationships, and encourage him/her to faith in Jesus Christ?

Parents: With God's help, we will.

Act of Dedication:

The minister may now take the child into his arms and say:

_____(Name)_____, we—your pastor and your parents— before this congregation dedicate you to God and to the service of his kingdom, in the name of the Father, Son, and Holy Spirit. (*The statement of dedication may be followed by a brief and specific prayer for the child and family.*)

At this point in the service, the parents may respond as the pastor returns the child, using these words as a model:

_____(Name)_____, we have dedicated you to the Lord for calling and service. God helping us, we promise to bring you up in the ways of the Lord. We will help you to know Jesus as your Savior, and we will seek to model the Christian walk before you.

Pastor (addressing the parents):

In recognition of the dedication of your child, I present to you (the parents) this New Testament inscribed with your child's name. From its pages instruct him/her in the way of life.

(continued on next page)

Charge to the Congregation
The minister may then address the congregation:

I charge you as members and friends to accept
_____(Name)_____ into the life of the congregation and to
share the responsibility for his/her nurture in Christ. As a
response of faith and commitment, will you as members of the
congregation stand as we pray. (*Follow with an appropriate
prayer.*)

An Alternative Rite of Child Dedication

Introduction
*The minister may select remarks preceding the dedication
vows or prepare his own. The following are optional:*

My friends, this is a happy and significant occasion which
brings us together. You have heard the words of the Master, "Let
the little children come to me, and do not hinder them, for the
kingdom of heaven belongs to such as these" (Matthew 19:14).
The young life which you hold in your arms is both a mystery and
a wonder. God has placed in your hearts a new and compelling
message of the dignity of life and the obligations of parenthood.

The Scriptures tell us of godly parents who dedicated their
children to the Lord and his service. Hannah brought her child
Samuel and dedicated him to God and to the service of his house.
Mary and Joseph brought Jesus as a child up to Jerusalem
according to the law of Moses, to present him to the Lord.

We are confident, therefore, of divine approval as this child
is brought this day to be dedicated to God and his service. It is our
duty as a Christian congregation to receive this child into the care
of the church, and to minister to his/her welfare in every way
possible.

God has a purpose for your child's life. To find that purpose
and to live it out fully will mean blessing; to refuse or ignore it will
mean failure. It is your privilege and duty to guide your child in
such a way as to make the will of God the greatest ambition of
his/her life.

To this task you are called to dedicate yourselves today; to
this end you dedicate your child to God.

Vows

   In place of the vows in the previous rite, the parents, under the guidance of the minister, may wish to prepare a personal statement of dedication and commitment to be spoken in unison or repeated after the minister phrase by phrase before the congregation.

Challenge to the Congregation

   The following may be printed in the bulletin as a challenge to the congregation:

   Minister: A congregation is a supportive community. By embodying the Spirit of Christ, a congregation provides love, support, direction, and meaning to persons within and without its membership. Today this body of Christ, the ___(Name of Congregation)___ congregation, is called to embrace ___(Name of child)___ and his/her parents in the arms of its care so that they may experience the power of God in their lives today and in the days and years to come. Will you respond with enthusiasm to this call?

   Congregational response: We will.

Recognition and Celebration of
A Newly-Born Baby in the Congregation

   The birth of a baby to parents who are not believers but are associated with the congregation may be recognized. The pastor should anticipate the first attendance of parents and child after the birth. During a sharing time in the service (or other appropriate time) an introduction of parents and child can be made, a rose presented to the parents, and a New Testament for the child with such words as:

   We celebrate the birth of ___(Name)___ and pray for God's blessings upon him/her as he/she enters the life of our congregation. Our duty and purpose is to surround ___(Name)___ and his/her family with Christian love and concern as you are all a part of this congregation. (*Prayer may be offered as appropriate.*)

Reception of New Members

Background and Preparation

A duty of the minister is to seek out those in the congregation who have turned from sin and unto God and who sincerely desire to follow Christ as Master and Lord, and to encourage such to publicly declare their faith and purpose by uniting with the church.

The Brethren in Christ have a heritage which has stressed a significant concept of the church. We perceive the church as a body of believers who are disciples and disciplined persons. That means we expect members of the church to be able to testify to a personal experience of God's saving grace, to be faithful to the principles of brotherhood as outlined in Matthew 18, to be Christians who exemplify obedience to Jesus Christ—including believers' baptism—and to be responsive to biblical moral standards.

Those considering membership in a Brethren in Christ congregation should have the benefit of proper preparation and counseling about what it means to have personal faith in Christ and what is expected of a Christian and a member of a Brethren in Christ Church. Often this is accomplished through membership classes or special instruction by the pastor.

Following such preparation and upon the satisfaction of the pastor that those desiring membership are truly believers in the Lord Jesus, the church board discusses the candidates and approves those who are to be received for membership. Their names are made known to the congregation at least one week before the service of reception. The candidates are then presented to the congregation at a regular worship service. At that time they may give public testimony of their faith in Christ or that may be done in conjunction with another service. At the appropriate time in the service, the minister asks the applicants to stand before him.

The Rite of Reception of Members

The pastor introduces the candidates for membership to the congregation and reminds the congregation that we welcome into membership those who have a personal experience of God's saving grace in Jesus Christ and who intend to live godly and holy lives. The pastor then asks the membership candidates to assent to a membership covenant:

Minister: Listen carefully as I present to you the covenant of membership by which you pledge your allegiance to God and fidelity to the church.

As a member of the Brethren in Christ Church, I accept the Bible as the Word of God in which is revealed the way of salvation and the guide for faith and conduct. I witness to a personal experience of God's saving grace in my heart, and express desire and purpose to live a holy life, apart from sin and separated unto Christ. I covenant as a member of the Brethren in Christ Church to be loyal to this congregation, to consent to instruction in Bible doctrine, to support and sustain the services of the congregation by my regular attendance and prayers, to contribute to the program of the church as the Lord prospers me, and to foster a spirit of Christian fellowship and oneness within the church.

If this is your purpose, will you affirm this covenant by answering, I do?

Applicants: I do.

Minister (to the congregation): You have heard the commitment these brothers and sisters are willing to make to you and to this church. Will you covenant with them to submit to one another out of reverence for Christ and to live a life of love toward one another just as Christ loved you and gave himself for you?

If so, will the members of this congregation please indicate this by standing?

Minister (having given the congregation opportunity to stand): Let us pray *(in the pastor's own words).*

(continued on next page)

Words of Reception and Greeting of New Members

Upon your testimony and acceptance of the membership covenant, we welcome you into the membership of this church with all the privileges and responsibilities associated.

With the words of reception it is appropriate to greet the new members. This may be done in a number of ways:

a. The minister may extend the right hand of fellowship to each, greeting with his own words or the following: On behalf of this congregation, I welcome you into its membership, in the name of the Father, Son, and Holy Spirit.

b. The pastor may shake hands or embrace each new member and welcome with appropriate words.

c. The pastor may present to each new member a verse from the Scriptures as a personal witness to commemorate this time. He may also present to each a New Testament, Bible, or appropriate book.

d. The pastor may invite members of the congregation to stand and pray for each new member; or he may invite members who have an especially close relation with the several new members to come forward and pray with each in the front of the church.

e. The church may plan a reception with a receiving line immediately after the service in which these people become members.

Benediction

An appropriate benediction such as Numbers 6:24-26 or Jude 24-25 may be offered if fitting at the given point in the total service.

Transfer of Members

Preparation

The use of letters of transfer when members change congregations within the denomination or from one denomination to another has widespread use in North America. When a transferring member brings a letter of transfer, the process is simple: After the potential member has submitted the letter and the pastor is satisfied of the person's standing in grace, the notice of the transfer can be read publicly and the member received with appropriate recognition. If a letter of transfer is not available, the pastor is encouraged to call the church most recently attended in pursuit of completion of the transfer of membership.

Practice is changing in many places regarding the transfer of members. In some instances the practice of letters of transfer is giving way generally to a rite of acceptance of persons on the basis of their Christian profession and testimony of relation to the church.

The pastor needs to open the door of the church to persons in sound Christian standing who have been members of another Christian denomination. Such persons should be invited to contact the pastor who will interview them regarding their Christian knowledge and faith; time, place, and mode of their baptism; and their present relation to God and to other people. A call by the pastor to the church most recently attended for recommendation is in order.

Also, some pastors and congregations ask that transferring members participate in a modified membership class.

When assured of the faith and standing of applicants, the pastor makes provision for a time of reception into membership on the basis of profession of faith. The pastor should inform the applicant of the pattern of the coming service so that there will be no surprises.

Rite of Transfer of Membership

The pastor may informally introduce the person(s) transferring into the congregation, briefly providing pertinent factual information. The applicant then presents a testimony of faith in Jesus Christ. Following the testimony the pastor says:

Pastor: You have here publicly confessed your faith in Jesus Christ as your Lord and Savior. You have witnessed to that faith in baptism. Do you now declare that it is your purpose to be a faithful member of this congregation, to submit to its authority, and to share in its ministries in keeping with the grace and gifts God gives you?

Response: I do.

Pastor (to the congregation): You have heard the commitment this (these) brother(s) and/or sister(s) is/are willing to make to you and to this church. Will you covenant with him/her/them to submit to one another out of reverence for Christ, and to live a life of love toward one another, just as Christ loved you and gave himself for you?

If so, will the members of this congregation please indicate this by standing?

After the congregation stands, the pastor addresses the candidate(s) for membership: As you have signified your desire to unite in worship, fellowship, and work with this congregation, on behalf of the church I welcome you, ⸻⸻⸻⸻⸻, in the name of the Lord Jesus Christ, and offer the right hand of fellowship. "Always give yourselves fully to the work of the Lord, because you know that your labor in the Lord is not in vain" (1 Corinthians 15:58).

Service of Restoration

In the human situation, it is possible that people turn from the Lord and fall into sin which results in a breaking of fellowship with the church. When this happens, the church is expected to reach out to seek to restore such persons; that is the nature and mission of Christ's church. When an erring church member repents and returns to the Lord, the church rejoices. It is appropriate to recognize the restoration of the fallen; in fact, it may well be a necessary and affirming act for repentant believers to openly confess their past sin and declare their repentant state. A service of restoration follows a period of suspension of membership or church discipline as deemed appropriate by the leadership of the church.

Rite of Restoration

Pastor: Scripture states: "If we confess our sins, he is faithful and just to forgive us our sins and to cleanse us from all unrighteousness" (1 John 1:9)._____(Name)_____, before the Lord and these brothers and sisters, do you profess that you truly repent of your sins and forsake them completely?

Response: I do.

Pastor (optional): Have you anything you wish to say to this congregation?

Response: (In the words of the penitent one.)

Pastor: Do you attest to your faith in Christ as your Lord and Savior and reaffirm your vows of faithfulness and service to the Lord and to his people in this congregation?

Response: I do.

Pastor: In behalf of your brothers and sisters, I offer you the right hand of fellowship, attesting the renewal of our relation in Christ with thanksgiving and declare the promise of Scripture: "If we walk in the light, as he is in the light, we have fellowship with one another, and the blood of Jesus, his Son, purifies us from every sin" (1 John 1:7).

Christian Marriage

There are few more significant opportunities for pastoral ministry than those that surround a wedding in the congregation. When a couple plans to be married, they are planning to bring together two families, two sets of values, two philosophies of life. The pastor stands at the meeting of these diverse streams. Opportunities abound to minister to both of the families involved, as well as to the emerging home.

Toward an Understanding of Marriage

In North American culture, marriage is both a secular and a sacred institution. The laws which govern marriage vary from state to state or from province to province, and the minister should become familiar with the laws in the particular area, realizing that while any marriage performed will be binding on the couple, the pastor may be open to prosecution if a marriage is performed outside the provisions of the local jurisdiction. This information is readily available from the clerk of courts or at the town hall.

Marriage is also a sacred institution, and where there is an awareness of this dimension the marriage is usually a service of worship. If the worship aspect of a marriage ceremony is kept clearly in focus, the preparation for the event and the rehearsal for the pageant itself will be appropriately influenced.

The Brethren in Christ Church affirms and teaches the sanctity of marriage. The church seeks to minister to all people including those whose "marital history and present status is not in accordance with the biblical standard which calls for the permanence of the marriage union, broken only by death" (*General Conference Minutes*, 1974, p. 25). Pastors should be familiar with the church's position on marriage and ministry to divorced persons as outlined in the *General Conference Minutes* (1974, pp. 24-28) and in the *Manual of Doctrine and Government*.

Preparation for Marriage

Pastors should be prepared to lead a couple planning to be married in several premarital counseling sessions. In the first of these sessions, the pastor should establish role expectations in preparation for the ceremony. It is usual in our culture for the bride's parents to finance the wedding celebration; hence, their wishes should be considered. The role of the bride and groom in preparation for the wedding ceremony should be clearly defined.

Premarital counseling will deal with the nuances of life together and the proper preparation for building a Christian home. Pastors who have not received training in this area in connection with their formal preparation for ministry will find help in the many books on the subject.

It is essential that a pastor help the couple to understand the spiritual resources available to persons who seek to build a harmonious home. Possible areas of marital tension should be discussed as creative opportunities, including finances, inter-family relationships, role expectations, values, sexual adjustments, and child rearing. While a great deal of time may not be spent on the above and similar subjects, raising these matters for discussion is helpful to the couple in understanding some of the responsibilities of marriage.

In preliminary conversation with the couple, it is well for the pastor to establish certain goals or purposes for the wedding. In this context pastors should emphasize the worship aspect of the marriage ceremony. The couple planning to be married may need to be alerted to the need to make relatives and friends comfortable at both the wedding ceremony and the reception. Details of the ceremony should be worked through carefully so that there are no regrets afterward.

A pastor is wise to design several check lists for use with regard to planning for a marriage ceremony. One check list may identify the participants and could provide a basis for understanding what each person sharing in the ceremony is expected to do and when they are expected to do it. Certain details regarding seating should be a part of this check list; in this way embarrassing moments are averted and the wedding party is made to feel at ease.

Another check list would focus on the actual processional and recessional: what music will be used, when does it begin, where do the participants come from, where do they stand, when does the father of the bride make his statement of presentation, etc.? Customs in these regards vary from congregation to congregation and should be known by the pastor prior to the first wedding in a new parish.

A third check list may deal with the reception. This check list is primarily for the help of the couple being married, but it also serves as a basis for pastoral ministry. A statement regarding the purpose of the reception should be given to the couple, and, if the reception is to be held in the church facilities, statements regarding policy, whom to phone for arrangements, custodial services, etc., should be included.

The Rehearsal

After carefully working through all details of the marriage ceremony, the pastor is usually asked to preside at the rehearsal. Most rehearsals will require approximately forty-five minutes if they are well planned and carefully carried out. The pastor will set the tone for the rehearsal by his introductory statements. A prayer for God's presence and guidance may be offered. Quiet insistence on careful observation of statements and actions will result in a wedding party feeling prepared for the ceremony. All of the aspects of the wedding ceremony should be carefully planned and rehearsed.

The Ceremony

Many couples like to have direct input into the ceremony itself and may wish to develop an order of service. The pastor will usually encourage such input, but will quietly insist on certain aspects of wedding vows and procedures being included.

Included here are two marriage ceremonies which may serve as models for the development of the service. A pastor may wish to share copies of one of these with the prospective bride and groom for their guidance.

Marriage Ceremony I

The ceremony begins at the hour announced on the wedding invitation; a musical program, if such is planned, usually precedes the stated hour. The persons to be married present themselves before the minister, the man at the left, the woman at the right of the minister.

Address to the Bride and Groom and to the Guests

Dear friends, we are assembled here in the presence of God to join this man and this woman in holy marriage, which is instituted by God, regulated by his commandments, blessed by our Lord Jesus Christ, and to be held in honor among all people. Let us, therefore, reverently remember that God has established and sanctified marriage for the welfare and happiness of humankind. Our Savior has declared that a man shall leave his father and mother and be united to his wife. By his apostles, he has instructed those who enter into this relation to cherish a mutual esteem and love; to bear with each other's infirmities and weaknesses; to comfort each other in sickness, trouble, and sorrow, in honesty and industry to provide for each other and for their household in temporal things; to pray for and encourage each other in the things which pertain to God; and to live together as heirs of the grace of life.

_____ and _____:
as you come to this altar before God, you have purposed to enter into Christian marriage. Christian marriage is unique: In commitment to God, you become one. In commitment to each other, this oneness is worked out through a lifetime. In Christian marriage, there is from here no looking back, no looking around. In Christ and the fellowship of his body, the Church, there is grace, wisdom, and support for you to grow and mature in life together in ever deepening dimensions.

Each of you brings to your marriage the gifts and endowments of your personalities, sex, and roles. May these complement one another in the enrichment of you both. Seek ways to give of yourselves to each other—not to get. Accept and cherish each other's gifts and talents as from the Lord. Keep the channels of communication open between you, for these are the avenues of joy and growth. Let not any day end with a wall standing between you. A good and blessed marriage does not just happen; it is made. Like a tender plant, a marriage grows strong when it is cultivated and nurtured with tender care and visible loving acts. Continually give yourselves to God and to each other. So shall your lives be rich together. The joys will be magnified, the sorrows modified, and the burdens made bearable.

(Addressing the congregation): As _____ and _____ come now to this place to be united in marriage, let us call upon God for guidance and blessing.

Prayer *(in the words of the minister, or as follows):*
Our Father in heaven, Lord of our lives today: We are assured that where two or three are gathered in Jesus' name, there he is among them. Grace this occasion with a sense of your presence, so that the words we say and the covenants we here declare may be under your Lordship. We worship you as we enter upon these responsible acts. In Jesus' name, Amen.

Commitment to Marriage
Minister: __(Groom's name)__, will you take __(Bride's name)__ to be your wedded wife, to cherish her and live with her according to God's holy ordinance? Will you pledge your loyalty to her, and promise to love, honor, comfort and keep her, in health and in sickness, in prosperity and adversity, and keep yourself unto her only so long as you both shall live? If so, answer I will.

Bridegroom: I will.

Minister: __(Bride's name)__, will you take __(Groom's name)__ to be your wedded husband, to cherish him and live with him according to God's holy ordinance? Will you pledge your loyalty to him, and promise to love, honor, comfort and keep him in health and in sickness, in prosperity and adversity, and keep yourself unto him only so long as you both shall live? If so, answer I will.

Bride: I will.

Giving of the Bride
Minister: Who gives this woman to be married to this man?
The person presenting the bride: I, (her father, guardian, brother, or friend), do. Or: Her mother and I do.

Repetition of Vows

(Vows may be memorized and recited, or repeated as follows):

_____(Groom's name)_____, will you take the hand of your bride and repeat after me this solemn covenant?

I, ____(Groom's name)____, take you _____(Bride's name)_____ to be my wedded wife, . . . to have and to hold from this day forward, . . . for better, for worse . . . for richer, for poorer . . . in sickness and in health . . . to love and to cherish . . . till death us do part . . . according to God's holy ordinance . . . and thereto I pledge you my faith. *(The couple releases their hands.)*

_____(Bride's name)_____, will you take the hand of your bridegroom and repeat after me this solemn covenant?

I, ____(Bride's name)____, take you _____(Groom's name)_____ to be my wedded husband, . . . to have and to hold from this day forward, . . . for better, for worse . . . for richer, for poorer . . . in sickness and in health . . . to love and to cherish . . . till death us do part . . . according to God's holy ordinance . . . and thereto I pledge you my faith. *(The couple releases their hands.)*

Exchange of Rings

Minister: ____(Groom's name)____, what token do you bring as a pledge that you will faithfully perform these vows?

Bridegroom (obtains ring from attendant, hands to minister and says): This ring.

Minister (holding ring): Let this ring be the sacred symbol of your abiding love. *(Returns the ring to the bridegroom.)*

Bridegroom (placing ring on the bride's finger): This ring I give you as a pledge of my abiding loyalty and love.

Minister: ____(Bride's name)____, what token do you bring as a pledge that you will faithfully perform these vows?

Bride (obtains ring from attendant, hands to minister and says): This ring.

Minister (holding ring): Let this ring be the sacred symbol of your abiding love. *(Returns the ring to the bride.)*

Bride (placing ring on the bridegroom's finger): This ring I give you as a pledge of my abiding loyalty and love.

Pronouncement of Marriage
Minister: _____ and _____,
join your right hands. *(Minister places his hand on their joined hands and says):*
Forasmuch as _____ and _____,
have consented together in holy marriage and have declared the same before God and in the presence of this company, I pronounce them husband and wife, in the name of the Father, and of the Son, and of the Holy Spirit. Amen. What God has joined together, let no one put asunder.

Prayer
(The bride and groom may kneel as the minister prays, concluding with an appropriate benediction.)

Conclusion
Minister: You may greet each other with a kiss. *Congratulations to the newly married couple by the minister. Then, turning to the congregation:* I present to their family and friends Mr. and Mrs. _____ _____.

Recessional

Marriage Ceremony II (Without the use of rings)

This ceremony is set in traditional language for those who may find this attractive for their vows. With the persons to be married standing together, the man to the right of the woman, the minister says:

Dearly beloved, we are gathered here in the presence of God, and with one another, to join this man and this woman in marriage, which is an honorable relationship, ordained of God in the very nature of our being, and designed for the happiness and welfare of mankind. This holy relationship is not to be entered into unadvisedly or lightly, but reverently, discreetly, soberly, and in the fear of God.

May I now call your attention to the words of Holy Scripture: Be subject to one another out of reverence for Christ. Wives, submit yourselves unto your own husbands, as unto the Lord. For the husband is the head of the wife, even as Christ is the head of the church. Therefore as the church is subject unto Christ, so let the wives be to their own husbands in everything. Husbands, love your wives, even as Christ also loved the church, and gave himself for it; so ought men to love their wives as their own bodies. He that loveth his wife loveth himself. For this cause shall a man leave his father and mother, and shall be joined unto his wife, and they two shall be one flesh (from Ephesians 5:21-31).

Prayer (The prayer may be as follows or in the minister's own words):

Almighty and ever-blessed heavenly Father, whose presence is the happiness of every condition, and whose favor hallows every relation: We beseech thee to be present and favorable unto these thy servants. As thou hast brought them together with thy providence, hallow now this service with thy presence, giving to them a oneness of heart fit for their new estate. Enrich them with all grace, whereby they may enjoy the comforts, undergo the cares, endure the trials, and perform the duties of life together as becometh Christians, under thy heavenly guidance and protection, through our Lord Jesus Christ. Amen.

(continued on next page)

Exchange of Vows

    *Minister (to the Bridegroom):*_____(Groom's name)_____,
do you now take_____(Bride's name)_____ to be your wife, to live
together after God's ordinance in the holy bond of marriage, and
will you promise in the presence of God and before these witnesses to love her and comfort her, honor and cherish her, in
sickness and in health, in prosperity and in adversity, and, forsaking all others, remain faithful to her as long as you both shall live?
If so, answer, I will.

    Bridegroom: I will.

    *Minister (to the Bride):*_____(Bride's name)_____, do you now
take_____(Groom's name)_____ to be your husband, to live together
after God's ordinance in the holy bond of marriage, and will you
promise in the presence of God and before these witnesses to love
him and comfort him, honor and cherish him, in sickness and in
health, in prosperity and in adversity, and, forsaking all others,
remain faithful to him as long as you both shall live? If so, answer
I will.

    Bride: I will.

Prayer *(as follows, or in the minister's own words):*
    Our loving heavenly Father, look mercifully upon these thy
servants, that they may love, honor, and cherish each other, and
so live together in faithfulness and patience, in wisdom and true
goodness, that their home may be a haven of blessing and peace;
through Jesus Christ our Lord, who liveth and reigneth with thee
and the Holy Spirit ever, one God, world without end. Amen.

Pronouncement of Marriage

_____and _____: will
you join your right hands? *(minister places his hand upon their
joined hands and says):*

    Those whom God has joined together, let not man put
asunder. Forasmuch as _____ and _____
have consented together in holy marriage, and have witnessed the
same before God and these friends, and thereto have given and
pledged their faith each to the other, and have declared the same

by joining hands, I pronounce that they are now husband and wife. In the name of the Father, and of the Son, and of the Holy Spirit. Amen.

Benediction

Now, may the blessing of our heavenly Father rest upon you, granting unto you all spiritual blessing in Christ Jesus. May God permit you to share together a long and happy and useful life here, and be made worthy to inherit all the joys of the heavenly life through Jesus Christ our Lord. Amen.

Ministry to the Sick

Facing Sickness

Sickness and affliction are a part of the human experience on this side of the Fall. Though we are in the time and place of the kingdom of God and authority is given over such things, we are in the interim: this is the time of "the altogether but not yet" regarding the kingdom. Much that is mysterious to us is present in these things. This should not keep us from approaching the Lord for healing and wholeness; on another hand, it does not give us the right to *demand* of God that he must heal. Rather, it gives us the right of approach, knowing that God has power to heal, that he does hear and respond to our appeal in his own way according to his perfect will.

We dare not imply that all sickness and hurt is the immediate result of personal sin. We dare not imply that the failure to receive healing is a mark of fault in the sick, a sign of lack of faith. We dare to come in trust, committing the sick to God, joining with them in faith, lifting them into the divine presence with assurance that God is doing what is good. The sick need assurance and confidence, not guilt and fear.

Illness is often a time of tenderness and particular openness to the ministrations of the gospel. We need to minister faithfully at such times, but we must not "press our advantage" by trying to manipulate people at a time of vulnerability. The pastor should develop a network of information within the congregation so that he hears of illness in it. He should call upon the sick as soon as propriety for such a call is indicated—and there are few reasons why a call upon the sick in a congregation would be omitted.

In preparing to visit the sick, the pastor must prepare his own spirit and mind for the situation at hand. He should not express shock or revulsion, no matter what he encounters. A glib or casual attitude with the sick or the family of the sick is inappropriate. Approaching with sensitivity and care, the thoughtful pastor will have the appropriate word of encouragement and cheer.

Visits to the sick should usually be brief, whether in home, hospital, or other facility. Inquire about the condition of the sick from those caring for them. Open the way for the sick to share fear, dread, or guilt with a question such as, "How are you feeling about this sickness?" or "Is there anything you want to tell me as your pastor just now?"

A reading of Scripture and a brief word of prayer complete the visit to the sick room. Some appropriate passages include the following: Psalms 23, 27, 46, 91, 103, 121; Isaiah 40; Matthew 6:25-33; John 14; Romans 8:26-39; 1 Corinthians 15:20-58; Hebrews 12:1-2; 1 Peter 4:12-19.

Prayer for the sick may be formal or informal; it may be accompanied by the laying on of hands, anointing with oil, or neither. There is scriptural precedent for any of these. (The minister needs to provide himself with a vial of olive oil for the anointing at such an occasion.) The purpose of this prayer is to give awareness that we are in the presence of God and that his resources are available to us.

The Rite of Anointing the Sick

The Epistle of James, 5:13-16, presents a picture of anointing the sick with oil for the healing of the body. The church sees this as an invitation for our participation with faith in God's power and will to heal. The service of healing may be in a home, a health institution, or congregation with an appropriate invitation to those who wish to participate. The following rite may be observed or adapted for a private or public service of anointing for healing. Generally, anointing is in response to the initiative of the sick person (see James 5:14).

Minister (in his own words or as follows): Words in the Epistle of James give you authority to call for the elders of the church to pray for you, that the Lord may raise you up. Hear the words of the Epistle, James 5:13-16:

"Is any one of you in trouble? He should pray. Is anyone happy? Let him sing songs of praise. Is any one of you sick? He should call the elders of the church to pray over him and anoint him with oil in the name of the Lord. And the prayer offered in faith will make the sick person well; the Lord will raise him up. If he has sinned, he will be forgiven. Therefore confess your sins to each other and pray for each other so that you may be healed. The prayer of a righteous man is powerful and effective."

The Scripture counsels that as we pray for healing, we should confess our sins that we may be forgiven. Are you aware of any sins that you would like to confess and put behind you?

(Here the individual may confess sins or give testimony to trust in the saving and cleansing merit of Christ. The minister should give assurance of forgiveness.)

Minister: Do you trust in Christ as your Savior and Healer? Are you ready to commit yourself to the hands of the Great Physician, trusting in his power to heal you?

Applicant: Yes.

Those participating in the rite draw near to pray and lay hands upon the sick as the minister prepares the vial of oil for the anointing.

Minister: _____, upon your request and on the authority of God's word for the strengthening of your faith and the healing of your body, I anoint you with oil in the name of the Lord. *(The minister places oil on his finger and applies it to the forehead of the applicant—in the pattern of the cross, if he wishes.)*

Fervent prayer is then offered for the sick with the laying on of hands by those participating. Thanks should be offered and trust expressed as the petition for healing is made in behalf of the sick. Let faith be expressed in the healing power and will of God and the sick encouraged to trust in Him. A blessing may be pronounced on the sick and those caring for him/her.

Ministry at the Time of Death

Pastoral Care of the Bereaved

The death of a member of the congregation affords the pastor an opportunity and challenge for ministry scarcely equalled in any other situation. It can bond the pastor with his people and open doors to relationship with those on the edges of the congregation. The empathy and compassion of the caring pastor will unite him with the people in their time of need.

As soon as practical after a death, the pastor should be in contact with the bereaved family; if possible, he will want to call at the affected home. This should be an unhurried time—a time to listen, to observe reactions, to continue sharing in the process of grieving. For these things, the pastor needs to hear and to sensitively discuss the positive aspects of the relationships of the bereaved with the deceased. The pastor will deliberately begin speaking of the deceased in the past tense. If it is the family's desire, the pastor will make himself available to assist with counsel or active involvement in making funeral arrangements in consultation with the funeral director regarding final arrangements.

The pastor will pray with and for the bereaved during the first visit and other visits as appropriate. A well-chosen, brief Scripture reading will begin focusing on the hope of the Christian faith.

The pastor will further minister to the family if he makes himself available to accompany the bereaved to the funeral home on their first visit after the preparation of the body.

Following the funeral service, committal, and other final activities, the pastor will wish to return to the home of the bereaved at an early date for a brief visit. Continuing pastoral care is essential for healthy adjustment to the loss.

Preparation for the Funeral Service

When the minister learns he will be responsible for the funeral service, he will confer with the bereaved to take into consideration the wishes of the deceased and the desires of the remaining family members. He will want to learn of any special wishes of the deceased and any desires of the immediate family relative to the funeral service such as selection of Scriptures, hymns, poetry, and special music. Local customs will influence the family's choices as to whether the service is held in the church or at the funeral home, whether ministers other than the pastor will participate, whether there will be hymns and special music. (Generally, the pastor of the local church where the deceased was a member conducts the funeral service.)

The funeral service should be brief and conducted with order and dignity. All aspects need to be planned carefully, allowing for local custom. A pastor in a new parish assignment will need to confer with the local funeral director(s) in his new community regarding custom about processional, recessional, and procedures at the cemetery.

In instances in which cremation of the remains is desired by the family, the service will need to be adapted according to the discretion of the pastor.

Purposes of the Funeral Service

The funeral service is planned both for worship and for healing. A key aspect of the worship experience is the focus on the hope the Christian faith offers. The celebration of hope will be a source of comfort for the bereaved. Hope at the time of death is a significant facet of the good news of the gospel.

The reading of Scriptures should form a central part of the funeral service. These should be well chosen and should communicate the comfort and support of the gospel. The prayers also are a source of comfort and healing at the time of the funeral. Some thought should be given to them in advance.

If the deceased was not a believer, the pastor's role is to be supportive to the loved ones without creating false hope. The message should be addressed to the living, pointing to the Lamb of God who takes away the sin of the world.

Funeral Services

Funeral practices differ in various parts of Canada and the United States. Along with this, there is increasing divergency in conducting final rites at the time of death. Offered here are services following a traditional approach and a suggestion for a memorial service.

The traditional service takes the pattern indicated here:
Organ Meditation
Opening Scripture Sentence or Call to Worship
Invocation
Hymn (read, or sung by congregation, soloist, or group)
Scripture Lesson
Prayer
Obituary and/or Words of Tribute (used less generally now)
Hymn (read, or sung by congregation, soloist, or group)
Meditation
Prayer
Benediction

In addition to the resources suggested in the following memorial services, other materials may be found in Section VII, pages 153-190.

Funeral Service I
Organ Meditation

Scripture Sentence (one or more of the following):
>   The eternal God is your refuge,
>   and underneath are the everlasting arms.
>   (Deuteronomy 33:27a)

>   The Lord is my light and my salvation—
>   whom shall I fear?
>   The Lord is the stronghold of my life—
>   of whom shall I be afraid? (Psalm 27:1)

>   As a father has compassion on his children,
>   so the Lord has compassion on those who fear him;
>   for he knows how we are formed,
>   he remembers that we are dust. (Psalm 103:13-14)

>   Now we know that if the earthly tent we live in is destroyed,
> we have a building from God, an eternal house in heaven, not
> built by human hands. (2 Corinthians 5:1)

Invocation (in the minister's own words or one of the following):
Almighty God, our Father, from whom we come, and unto whom our spirits return: You have been our dwelling place in all generations. You are our refuge and strength, a very present help in trouble. Grant us your blessing in this hour, and enable us so to put our trust in you, that our spirits may grow calm and our hearts be comforted. Lift our eyes beyond the shadows of earth, and help us to see the light of eternity. So may we find grace and strength for this and every time of need; through Jesus Christ our Lord. Amen.

Our Father who is in Heaven, and our Father who is here now, look upon us in our need with grace and consolation. We are assured that you do not willingly grieve or afflict people; compassion and mercy are your qualities. Be near your servants, especially this bereaved home, whose joy is turned into mourning. According to your great mercy, be pleased to uphold, strengthen, and comfort the sorrowing, that they may not be overwhelmed in their anguish. Rather, may we all find in you our strength and refuge and commit ourselves anew to you with confidence and hope that our times are in your hands, through Christ our Lord. Amen.

Hymn

If the life of the deceased has been a strong Christian testimony, the hymn selections may well be ones of victory and triumph. If the funeral is in a church, these will be sung by the congregation. If the service is in a funeral home, the minister may choose to read the hymn or have it sung by a soloist or group.

Scripture Lesson

Here the minister will read selected passages which address the Christian hope, the call of the gospel, and counsel in times of need. Following are several appropriate portions from the Old and New Testaments.

The Lord is my shepherd, I shall lack nothing.
He makes me lie down in green pastures,
he leads me beside quiet waters,
he restores my soul.
He guides me in paths of righteousness
for his name's sake.
Even though I walk
through the valley of the shadow of death,
I will fear no evil,
for you are with me;
your rod and your staff,
they comfort me.
You prepare a table before me
in the presence of my enemies.
You anoint my head with oil;
my cup overflows.
Surely goodness and love will follow me
all the days of my life,
and I will dwell in the house of the Lord forever.
(Psalm 23)

Lord, you have been our dwelling place
throughout all generations.
Before the mountains were born
or you brought forth the earth and the world,
from everlasting to everlasting you are God.

For a thousand years in your sight
    are like a day that has just gone by,
    or like a watch in the night.
                (Psalm 90:1-2, 4)

God is our refuge and strength,
    an ever present help in trouble.
Therefore we will not fear, though the earth give way
    and the mountains fall into the heart of the sea,
though its waters roar and foam
    and the mountains quake with their surging. Selah
                (Psalm 46:1-3)

I tell you the truth, whoever hears my word and believes him who sent me has eternal life and will not be condemned; he has crossed over from death to life. I tell you the truth, a time is coming and has now come when the dead will hear the voice of the Son of God and those who hear will live. For as the Father has life in himself, so he has granted the Son to have life in himself. And he has given him authority to judge because he is the Son of Man.

Do not be amazed at this, for a time is coming when all who are in their graves will hear his voice and come out—those who have done good will rise to live, and those who have done evil will rise to be condemned.
                (John 5:24-29)

Do not let your hearts be troubled. Trust in God; trust also in me. In my Father's house are many rooms; if it were not so, I would have told you. I am going there to prepare a place for you. And if I go and prepare a place for you, I will come back and take you to be with me that you also may be where I am. You know the way to the place where I am going.

Thomas said to him, "Lord, we don't know where you are going, so how can we know the way?"

Jesus answered, "I am the way and the truth and the life. No one comes to the Father except through me."
                (John 14:1-6)

But if it is preached that Christ has been raised from the dead, how can some of you say that there is no resurrection of the dead? If there is no resurrection of the dead, then not even Christ has been raised. And if Christ has not been raised, our preaching is useless and so is your faith. More than that, we are then found to be false witnesses about God, for we have testified about God that he raised Christ from the dead. But he did not raise him if in fact the dead are not raised. For if the dead are not raised, then Christ has not been raised either. And if Christ has not been raised, your faith is futile; you are still in your sins. Then those also who have fallen asleep in Christ are lost. If only for this life we have hope in Christ, we are to be pitied more than all men.

But Christ has indeed been raised from the dead, the first-fruits of those who have fallen asleep. For since death came through a man, the resurrection of the dead comes also through a man. For as in Adam all die, so in Christ all will be made alive. But each in his own turn: Christ, the firstfruits; then, when he comes, those who belong to him. Then the end will come, when he hands over the kingdom to God the Father after he has destroyed all dominion, authority and power. For he must reign until he has put all his enemies under his feet. The last enemy to be destroyed is death.

(1 Corinthians 15:12-26)

Praise be to the God and Father of our Lord Jesus Christ! In his great mercy he has given us new birth into a living hope through the resurrection of Jesus Christ from the dead, and into an inheritance that can never perish, spoil or fade—kept in heaven for you, who through faith are shielded by God's power until the coming of the salvation that is ready to be revealed in the last time. In this you greatly rejoice, though now for a little while you may have had to suffer grief in all kinds of trials. These have come so that your faith—of greater worth than gold, which perishes even though refined by fire—may be proved genuine and may result in praise, glory and honor when Jesus Christ is revealed. Though you have not seen him, you love him; and even though you do not see him now, you believe in him and are filled with an inexpressible and glorious joy, for you are receiving the goal of your faith, the salvation of your souls.

(1 Peter 1:3-9)

After this I looked and there before me was a great multitude that no one could count, from every nation, tribe, people and language, standing before the throne and in front of the Lamb.

They were wearing white robes and were holding palm branches in their hands. And they cried out in a loud voice:

"Salvation belongs to our God,
who sits on the throne,
and to the Lamb."

All the angels were standing around the throne and around the elders and the four living creatures. They fell down on their faces before the throne and worshiped God, saying:

"Amen!
Praise and glory
and wisdom and thanks and honor
and power and strength
be to our God for ever and ever.
Amen!"

Then one of the elders asked me, "These in white robes—who are they, and where did they come from?"

I answered, "Sir, you know."

And he said, "These are they who have come out of the great tribulation; they have washed their robes and made them white in the blood of the Lamb. Therefore,

"they are before the throne of God
and serve him day and night in his temple;
and he who sits on the throne will spread his tent over them.
Never again will they hunger;
never again will they thirst.
The sun will not beat upon them,
nor any scorching heat.

For the Lamb at the center of the throne will be their shepherd;
he will lead them to springs of living water.
And God will wipe away every tear from their eyes."

(Revelation 7:9-17)

Prayer

In the words of the minister, suitable for the circumstances and the occasion.

Obituary and/or Tributes

Obituaries are read less frequently now than in previous times. The minister consults with the family in this regard. If the deceased was widely known and of prominent standing, tributes may be appropriate. The obituary is prepared by the family, possibly with the help of the minister. Tributes are prepared by appropriate representatives of agencies of which the deceased was a part.

Hymn
Sung by the congregation or a special group, or read by the minister.

Message
The message or meditation is usually brief (ten to fifteen minutes), scriptural, and appropriate for the circumstances and the occasion.

Prayer *(in the words of the minister or as follows):*
O Lord and Master, who yourself wept beside the grave: we have seen that you are touched with the feeling of our sorrows: fulfill now your promise that you will not leave your people comfortless, but you will come to them. Reveal yourself unto your sorrowing servants, and cause them to hear you say, "I am the resurrection and the life." Help these who have lost a loved one to turn to you with true discernment, and to abide in you through living faith, that, finding now the comfort of your presence, they may have also a sure confidence in you for all that is to come; until the day break, and the shadows flee away. Hear us by your great and abiding mercy, O Jesus Christ our Lord. Amen.

Benediction
May the God of peace, who through the blood of the eternal covenant brought back from the dead our Lord Jesus, that great Shepherd of the sheep, equip you with everything good for doing his will, and may he work in us what is pleasing to him, through Jesus Christ, to whom be glory for ever and ever. Amen. (Hebrews 13:20-21)

Funeral Service II

The minister shall say:
Jesus said, "I am the resurrection and the life. He who believes in me will live, even though he dies; and whoever lives and believes in me will never die."

"Come to me, all you who are weary and burdened, and I will give you rest. Take my yoke upon you and learn from me, for I am gentle and humble in heart, and you will find rest for your souls."

Let us pray.

Prayer (in the minister's own words or as follows):
Almighty God, your love never fails. Only you can turn the shadow of death into daybreak. Enable us to receive your word with believing hearts, so that your promises may come alive to us in this our time of need. Give us your hope that we may be lifted into the light and peace of your presence; through Jesus Christ our Lord. Amen.

Or,
Our Father, who art in heaven, be our refuge and strength in this our time of need, that as we hold to your word, we may be strong in your grace; through Jesus Christ our Lord. Amen.

Hymn
This may be read by the minister, sung by the congregation, or sung by a person or group called for this purpose.

Scripture
Selecting from one of the following Scriptures, the minister shall say: Hear now the reading of the Scriptures:

Lord, you have been our dwelling place
throughout all generations.
Before the mountains were born
or you brought forth the earth and the world,
from everlasting to everlasting you are God.
You turn men back to dust,
saying, "Return to dust, O sons of men."
For a thousand years in your sight
are like a day that has just gone by,
or like a watch in the night.

You sweep men away in the sleep of death;
    they are like the new grass in the morning—
though in the morning it springs up new,
    by evening it is dry and withered. . . .
Relent, O Lord! How long will it be?
    Have compassion on your servants.
Satisfy us in the morning with your unfailing love,
    that we may sing for joy and be glad all our days.
Make us glad for as many days as you have afflicted us,
    for as many years as we have seen trouble.
May your deeds be shown to your servants,
    your splendor to their children.
May the favor of the Lord our God rest upon us;
    establish the work of our hands for us—
    yes, establish the work of our hands.
               (Psalm 90:1-6, 13-17)

Man born of woman
    is of few days and full of trouble.
He springs up like a flower and withers away;
    like a fleeting shadow, he does not endure. . .
Man's days are determined;
    you have decreed the number of his months
    and have set limits he cannot exceed.
So look away from him and let him alone,
    till he has put in his time like a hired man.
At least there is hope for a tree:
    If it is cut down, it will sprout again,
    and its new shoots will not fail.
Its roots may grow old in the ground
    and its stump die in the soil,
yet at the scent of water it will bud
    and put forth shoots like a plant.
But man dies and is laid low;
    he breathes his last and is no more.
               (Job 14:1-2, 5-10)

O Lord, you have searched me
    and you know me.
You know when I sit and when I rise;
    you perceive my thoughts from afar.

You discern my going out and my lying down;
   you are familiar with all my ways.
Before a word is on my tongue
   you know it completely, O Lord. . . .
Where can I go from your Spirit?
   Where can I flee from your presence?
If I go up to the heavens, you are there;
   if I make my bed in the depths, you are there.
If I rise on the wings of the dawn,
   if I settle on the far side of the sea,
even there your hand will guide me,
   your right hand will hold me fast.
If I say, "Surely the darkness will hide me
   and the light become night around me,"
even the darkness will not be dark to you;
   the night will shine like the day,
   for darkness is as light to you. . . .
How precious to me are your thoughts, O God!
   How vast is the sum of them!
Were I to count them,
   they would outnumber the grains of sand.
When I awake,
   I am still with you. . . .
Search me, O God, and know my heart;
   test me and know my anxious thoughts.
See if there is any offensive way in me,
   and lead me in the way everlasting.
(Psalm 139:1-4, 7-12, 17-18, 23-24)

It is written: "I believed; therefore I have spoken." With that same spirit of faith we also believe and therefore speak, because we know that the one who raised the Lord Jesus from the dead will also raise us with Jesus and present us with you in his presence. All this is for your benefit, so that the grace that is reaching more and more people may cause thanksgiving to overflow to the glory of God.

Therefore we do not lose heart. Though outwardly we are wasting away, yet inwardly we are being renewed day by day. For our light and momentary troubles are achieving for us an eternal glory that far outweighs them all. So we fix our eyes not on what is seen, but on what is unseen. For what is seen is temporary, but what is unseen is eternal.

Now we know that if the earthly tent we live in is destroyed, we have a building from God, an eternal house in heaven, not built by human hands. Meanwhile we groan, longing to be clothed with our heavenly dwelling, because when we are clothed, we will not be found naked. For while we are in this tent, we groan and are burdened, because we do not wish to be unclothed but to be clothed with our heavenly dwelling, so that what is mortal may be swallowed up by life. Now it is God who has made us for this very purpose and has given us the Spirit as a deposit, guaranteeing what is to come.

(2 Corinthians 4:13—5:5)

Brothers, we do not want you to be ignorant about those who fall asleep, or to grieve like the rest of men, who have no hope. We believe that Jesus died and rose again and so we believe that God will bring with Jesus those who have fallen asleep in him. According to the Lord's own word, we tell you that we who are still alive, who are left till the coming of the Lord, will certainly not precede those who have fallen asleep. For the Lord himself will come down from heaven, with a loud command, with the voice of the archangel and with the trumpet call of God, and the dead in Christ will rise first. After that, we who are still alive and are left will be caught up with them in the clouds to meet the Lord in the air. And so we will be with the Lord forever. Therefore encourage each other with these words.

(1 Thessalonians 4:13-18)

We know that in all things God works for the good of those who love him, who have been called according to his purpose. . . . What, then, shall we say in response to this? If God is for us, who can be against us? He who did not spare his own Son, but gave him up for us all—how will he not also, along with him, graciously give us all things? Who will bring any charge against those whom God has chosen? It is God who justifies. Who is he that condemns? Christ Jesus, who died—more than that, who was raised to life—is at the right hand of God and is also interceding for us. Who shall separate us from the love of Christ? Shall trouble or hardship or persecution or famine or nakedness or danger or sword? As it is written:
  "For your sake we face death all day long;
    we are considered as sheep to be slaughtered."
No, in all these things we are more than conquerors through him who loved us. For I am convinced that neither death nor life,

neither angels nor demons, neither the present nor the future, nor any powers, neither height nor depth, nor anything else in all creation, will be able to separate us from the love of God that is in Christ Jesus our Lord.

(Romans 8:28-39)

For this reason I kneel before the Father, from whom his whole family in heaven and on earth derives its name. I pray that out of his glorious riches he may strengthen you with power through his Spirit in your inner being, so that Christ may dwell in your hearts through faith. And I pray that you, being rooted and established in love, may have power, together with all the saints, to grasp how wide and long and high and deep is the love of Christ, and to know this love that surpasses knowledge—that you may be filled to the measure of all the fullness of God.

Now to him who is able to do immeasurably more than all we ask or imagine, according to his power that is at work within us, to him be glory in the church and in Christ Jesus throughout all generations, for ever and ever! Amen.

(Ephesians 3:14-19)

Prayer *(in the minister's own words or as follows):*
Eternal God, our Father, we offer thanks for your word which is a light to us in the darkness. May we hear its truth and may it bring us light and hope now and in the time to come.

Hymn
This may be read by the minister or sung by the congregation or by a person or group called for that purpose.

Sermon
The minister may now preach a brief sermon testifying to the hope of the Christian faith.

Prayer and Benediction *(in the minister's own words, or as follows:)*
We believe there is now no condemnation for those who are in Christ Jesus: and we know that in everything God works for good with those who love him, who are called according to his purpose. We are sure that neither death, nor life, nor angels, nor principalities, nor things present, nor things to come, nor powers, nor height, nor depth, nor anything else in all creation, will be able to separate us from the love of God in Christ Jesus our Lord.

The peace of God which passes all understanding keep your hearts and minds in the knowledge and love of God, and of His Son Jesus Christ, our Lord. Amen.

Funeral Service III—For a Child

Organ Meditation

Scripture *(select appropriate verses from the following):*
God is our refuge and strength,
an ever present help in trouble. . . .
As a father has compassion on his children,
so the Lord has compassion on those who fear him.
(Psalm 46:1, Psalm 103:13)

People were bringing little children to Jesus to have him touch them, but the disciples rebuked them. When Jesus saw this, he was indignant. He said to them, "Let the little children come to me, and do not hinder them, for the kingdom of God belongs to such as these. I tell you the truth, anyone who will not receive the kingdom of God like a little child will never enter it." And he took the children in his arms, put his hands on them and blessed them.
(Mark 10:13-16)

Invocation *(in the words of the minister or as follows):*
Our Father in heaven, you have made no life in vain, and you love all that you have made. In our sorrow grant us your loving presence to comfort and sustain us in this time of our need. Speak to the waiting hearts grievously stricken in this time: answer their questioning, quicken their faith, give solace for their sorrow, and grant them courage for this and all the days that are to come; through Jesus Christ our Lord. Amen.

The Lord's Prayer
The minister may pray the prayer or the congregation may be invited to join in praying the Lord's Prayer at the conclusion of the invocation.

Scripture *(the minister here reads selections from the following Scriptures):*

The Lord is my shepherd, I shall lack nothing.
He makes me lie down in green pastures,
he leads me beside quiet waters,
    he restores my soul.
He guides me in paths of righteousness
    for his name's sake.
Even though I walk
    through the valley of the shadow of death,
I will fear no evil,
    for you are with me;
your rod and your staff,
    they comfort me.
You prepare a table before me
    in the presence of my enemies.
You anoint my head with oil;
    my cup overflows.
Surely goodness and love will follow me
    all the days of my life,
and I will dwell in the house of the Lord forever.
(Psalm 23)

You who bring good tidings to Zion,
    go up on a high mountain.
You who bring good tidings to Jerusalem,
    lift up your voice with a shout,
lift it up, do not be afraid;
    say to the towns of Judah,
    "Here is your God!"
See, the Sovereign Lord comes with power,
    and his arm rules for him.
See, his reward is with him,
    and his recompense accompanies him.
He tends his flock like a shepherd:
    He gathers the lambs in his arms
and carries them close to his heart;
    he gently leads those that have young.
(Isaiah 40:9-11)

At that time the disciples came to Jesus and asked, "Who is the greatest in the kingdom of heaven?"

He called a little child and had him stand among them. And he said: "I tell you the truth, unless you change and become like little children, you will never enter the kingdom of heaven. Therefore, whoever humbles himself like this child is the greatest in the kingdom of heaven. And whoever welcomes a little child like this in my name welcomes me. . . .

"See that you do not look down on one of these little ones. For I tell you that their angels in heaven always see the face of my Father in heaven. . . . Your Father in heaven is not willing that any of these little ones should be lost."

(Matthew 18:1-5, 10, 14)

Sermon

The sermon should be appropriate for the occasion, being both simple and brief.

Poem

A hymn or poem is read by the minister.

Prayer and Benediction *(in the minister's own words or as follows):*

Father of mercies and God of all comfort, look in pity on these your servants whose joy has been turned into sorrow. They have drunk of the cup of bitterness; be pleased, we pray, to give them the cup of consolation. Let not their faith falter nor their light go out in darkness. Give them the spirit of him who learned obedience by the things he suffered, so that like him, they too may in submission say, "Not my will but thine be done." Comfort them with the assurance that their loved one is at rest in you and will be remembered in the day when you make up your treasured possession (Malachi 3:17). In this hour of trial, draw your servants close to your love and help them to trust in you and to believe that stronger than the pain and the mystery of death are the everlasting arms of your tender mercy. Hear our prayer for the sake of him who is our only Mediator and Advocate, our Savior, Jesus Christ. Amen.

The Lord bless you and keep you. The Lord make his face shine upon you and be gracious unto you. The Lord lift up his countenance upon you and give you peace, through Jesus Christ our Lord. Amen.

A Memorial Service
(Following a Private Service of Committal)

As early as appropriate following death, when the remains have been prepared for burial or cremation, the minister and family, along with any persons designated by the family, will gather in the funeral home or cemetery for a service of committal. This will generally follow the pattern of one of the committal services below with some expansion in words of comfort and assurance to the bereaved. The remains will be cared for according to the plans determined by the family and a public memorial service will be planned and announced for the congregation of which the deceased had been a part.

The memorial service will be a service of worship, emphasizing the Christian hope and the assurance of eternal life in Jesus Christ.

Scripture Sentences
Jesus said, "I am the way, the truth and the life. No man comes to the Father except through me. . . . I am the resurrection and the life. He who believes in me will live, even though he dies; and whoever lives and believes in me will never die."

"Do not let your hearts be troubled. Trust in God; trust also in me. In my Father's house are many rooms; if it were not so, I would have told you. I am going there to prepare a place for you. And if I go and prepare a place for you, I will come back and take you to be with me that you also may be where I am."

Prayer (in the minister's own words or as follows):
Almighty God, whose love never fails, and who can turn the shadow of death into daybreak: help us to receive your word with believing hearts, so that, hearing the promises in Scripture, we may have hope and be lifted out of darkness into the light and peace of your presence; through Jesus Christ our Lord. Amen.

Hymn
This may be read by the minister, sung by the congregation, or sung by a person or group called for this purpose.

Words may be spoken here addressing the purpose of the occasion. These may introduce the nature and purpose of this memorial service. They may further recall the life of the departed in some of the facts about the life and contributions of the deceased and words of appreciation.

Scriptures

In this hour of our need the Scriptures bring us comfort, counsel and hope. Let us turn to them together in this memorial service. *(Select from the following):*

Out of the depths I cry to you, O Lord;
    O Lord, hear my voice.
Let your ears be attentive
    to my cry for mercy.
If you, O Lord, kept a record of sins,
    O Lord, who could stand?
But with you there is forgiveness;
    therefore you are feared.
I wait for the Lord, my soul waits,
    and in his word I put my hope.
My soul waits for the Lord
    more than watchmen wait for the morning.
O Israel, put your hope in the Lord,
    for with the Lord is unfailing love
    and with him is full redemption.
He himself will redeem Israel
    from all their sins.
                 (Psalm 130)

Praise the Lord, O my soul;
    all my inmost being, praise his holy name.
Praise the Lord, O my soul,
    and forget not all his benefits.
He forgives all my sins
    and heals all my diseases;
he redeems my life from the pit
    and crowns me with love and compassion. . . .
For as high as the heavens are above the earth,
    so great is his love for those who fear him;
as far as the east is from the west,
    so far has he removed our transgressions from us.
As a father has compassion on his children,
    so the Lord has compassion on those who fear him;

for he knows how we are formed,
>   he remembers that we are dust.
As for man, his days are like grass,
>   he flourishes like a flower of the field;
the wind blows over it and it is gone,
>   and its place remembers it no more.
But from everlasting to everlasting
>   the Lord's love is with those who fear him,
>   and his righteousness with their children's children—
with those who keep his covenant
>   and remember to obey his precepts. . . .
Praise the Lord, O my soul.

(Psalm 103:1-4, 11-18, 22)

What shall we say, then? Shall we go on sinning so that grace may increase? By no means! We died to sin; how can we live in it any longer? Or don't you know that all of us who were baptized into Christ Jesus were baptized into his death? We were therefore buried with him through baptism into death in order that, just as Christ was raised from the dead through the glory of the Father, we too may live a new life.

If we have been united with him in his death, we will certainly also be united with him in his resurrection. . . . Now if we died with Christ, we believe that we will also live with him. For we know that since Christ was raised from the dead, he cannot die again; death no longer has mastery over him. The death he died, he died to sin once for all; but the life he lives, he lives to God.

(Romans 6:1-5, 8-10)

Christ has indeed been raised from the dead, the firstfruits of those who have fallen asleep. For since death came through a man, the resurrection of the dead comes also through a man. For as in Adam all die, so in Christ all will be made alive. . . .

I declare to you, brothers, that flesh and blood cannot inherit the kingdom of God, nor does the perishable inherit the imperishable. Listen, I tell you a mystery: We will not all sleep, but we will all be changed—in a flash, in the twinkling of an eye, at the last trumpet. For the trumpet will sound, the dead will be raised imperishable, and we will be changed. For the perishable must clothe itself with the imperishable, and the mortal with immortality. When the perishable has been clothed with the imperishable, and the mortal with immortality, then the saying that is written will come true: "Death has been swallowed up in victory."

"Where, O death, is your victory?
Where, O death, is your sting?"
The sting of death is sin, and power of sin is the law. But thanks be to God! he gives us the victory through our Lord Jesus Christ.

(1 Corinthians 15:20-22, 50-57)

For this reason I kneel before the Father, from whom his whole family in heaven and on earth derives its name. I pray that out of his glorious riches he may strengthen you with power through his Spirit in your inner being, so that Christ may dwell in your hearts through faith. And I pray that you, being rooted and established in love, may have power, together with all the saints to grasp how wide and long and high and deep is the love of Christ, and to know this love that surpasses knowledge—that you may be filled to the measure of all the fullness of God.

Now to him who is able to do immeasurably more than all we ask or imagine, according to his power that is at work within us, to him be glory in the church and in Christ Jesus throughout all generations, for ever and ever! Amen.

(Ephesians 3:14-19)

Prayer *(in the minister's own words with thanksgiving for our hope in Christ and lifting the bereaved to the Lord for support; or in the following words):*
Eternal God, our Father, we offer thanks for your Word which is a light to us in the darkness. May we hear its truth and may it bring us assurance and hope now and in the time to come.

Hymn
Read by the minister or sung by the congregation or by a person or group called for that purpose. Or the minister may read a poem of his selection.

Sermon
The minister may now preach a brief message testifying to the hope of the Christian faith and comforting the hearts of those present.

(continued on next page)

Prayer and Benediction

The minister leads in prayer and a benediction as follows or in his own words:

O God, before whom generations rise and pass away: we praise you for all your servants who, having lived this life in faith, now live eternally with you. Especially we thank you for your servant _____, for the gift of his/her life, for the grace you have given, for all in him/her that was good and kind and faithful. *(Here mention may be made of characteristics or service.)* We thank you that for him/her, death is past and pain is ended, and he/she has entered the joy you have prepared; through Jesus Christ our Lord. Amen.

Peace I leave with you; my peace I give to you; not as the world gives do I give to you. Let not your hearts be troubled, neither let them be afraid.

The grace of the Lord Jesus Christ, and the love of God, and the fellowship of the Holy Spirit, be with you all. Amen.

Committal Service I

Words of Comfort and Assurance

With the people assembled at the final resting place, the minister may say:

Standing beside this open grave, hear once more the words of Scripture:

Brothers, we do not want you to be ignorant about those who fall asleep, or to grieve like the rest of men, who have no hope. We believe that Jesus died and rose again and so we believe that God will bring with Jesus those who have fallen asleep in him. According to the Lord's own word, we tell you that we who are still alive, who are left till the coming of the Lord, will certainly not precede those who have fallen asleep. For the Lord himself will come down from heaven, with a loud command, with the voice of the archangel and with the trumpet call of God, and the dead in Christ will rise first. After that, we who are still alive and are left will be caught up with them in the clouds to meet the Lord in the air. And so we will be with the Lord forever. Therefore encourage each other with these words. (1 Thessalonians 4:13-18)

Committal Prayer (in the minister's own words or as follows):

Our Father, we look to you again, facing this moment of our need. In our sorrow, grief, and loneliness, draw us up to yourself that we may know the comfort of the everlasting arms. Especially support and comfort those who have been closest to our departed brother/sister. Sustain them in the blessed assurance that death is conquered, the new life is begun; to be absent from the body is to be present with the Lord. May we be assured in the hope that we shall walk together again in your blessed presence. Help us to number our days that we may apply our hearts unto wisdom. Through Jesus Christ our Lord. Amen.

Words of Committal

And now, forasmuch as the spirit of the departed has entered into the life immortal, we therefore commit his/her body to its resting place, but his/her spirit we commend to God in assurance that he does all things well. For we know that if the earthly tent we live in is destroyed, we have a building from God, an eternal house in heaven, not built by human hands.

Benediction

The grace of our Lord Jesus Christ, and the love of God, and the communion of the Holy Spirit, be with us all, evermore. Amen.

Committal Service II

When all are assembled, let the minister say:
Thank God, the God and Father of our Lord Jesus Christ, that in his great mercy we have been born again into a life full of hope, through Christ's rising from the dead.
Do not be afraid. I am the first and the last. I am the living one; for I was dead and now I am alive for evermore.
Because I live, you shall live also.
Almighty God: we commend to you our friend and neighbor, _____, trusting your love and mercy and believing in the promise of a resurrection to eternal life, through our Lord Jesus Christ. Amen.
All thanks to God who gives us the victory through our Lord Jesus Christ!

Prayer (in the minister's words or one of the following prayers):
O Lord: support us all the day long, until the shadows lengthen and the evening comes, and the busy world is hushed, and the fever of life is over, and our work is done. Then, in your mercy, grant us a safe lodging, and a holy rest, and peace at the last, through Jesus Christ our Lord. Amen.

O God: you have designed this wonderful world and provide all things good for us. Give us such faith that by day and by night, in all times and in all places we may without fear trust those who are dear to us to your never-failing love, in this life and in the life to come; through Jesus Christ our Lord. Amen.

Eternal God: our days and years are lived in your mercy. Make us know how frail we are, and how brief our time on earth; and lead us by your Holy Spirit, so that, when we have served you in our generation, we may be gathered into your presence, faithful in the church, and loving toward neighbors; through Jesus Christ our Lord. Amen.

Father: you gave your own Son Jesus to die on the cross for us, and raised him from death as a sign of your love. Give us faith, so that, though our child has died, we may believe that you welcome him/her and will care for him/her, until, by your mercy, we are together again in the joy of your promised kingdom, through Jesus Christ our Lord. Amen.

Benediction *(the minister may offer a benediction in his own words or as follows):*
Now, may the grace of our Lord Jesus Christ, the love of God, and the communion of the Holy Spirit be with us all. Amen.

Committal Service III

At the grave, when the people are assembled, the minister shall say one or more of the following sentences:
As a father has compassion on his children, so the Lord has compassion on those who fear him. (Psalm 103:13)

From everlasting to everlasting the Lord's love is with those who fear him, and his righteousness with their children's children. (Psalm 103:17)

Our help is in the name of the Lord, the maker of heaven and earth. (Psalm 124:8)

Say to those with fearful hearts, "Be strong, do not fear; your God will come . . . to save you." (Isaiah 35:4)

Then the minister will say:
Dear friends, we have gone as far as human hands can perform, and as far as mortal feet can follow. We have entered the quiet city of the dead, and we have surrounded the open tomb. We have paid the last tribute of respect to our dear departed. This once more reminds us that we are only sojourners here, and that we are but passing mortals, and as God has said, we shall return to the earth from whence we have been taken.

Because the spirit of the departed has returned to God who gave it, we now commit the body to the ground, the earthly to the earth. We are looking for the general resurrection in the last day and life in the world to come, through our Lord Jesus Christ. At his coming in glorious majesty to judge the world, the earth and the sea shall give up their dead. The corruptible bodies of those who sleep in him shall be changed and made like him in his own glorious body. This he accomplishes according to the mighty working of his power whereby he is able to subdue all things unto himself.

93

Then the minister will say:

I heard a voice from heaven, saying unto me: Blessed are the dead who die in the Lord from henceforth: Yea, saith the Spirit, that they may rest from their labors; and their works do follow them.

Then the minister may offer one or more of the following prayers, or may pray in his/her own words:

Our Father in Heaven: We come to you in the name of your Son Jesus. We grasp and hold to the assurances he has given us: "I am the resurrection and the life. He who believes in me will live, even though he dies; and whoever lives and believes in me will never die" (John 11:25-26). Raise us, Father, we pray, from the death of sin into the life of righteousness by grace through faith. Prepare us, that when we depart this life, we may rest in Jesus and may receive through him that blessing which he has pronounced to all that love him, saying, "Come, you who are blessed by my Father, take your inheritance, the kingdom prepared for you since the creation of the world." Our prayer is in the name of Jesus, your Son, and our Savior. Amen.

Almighty God, by the death of your own dear Son, Jesus Christ, you have destroyed death. By his rest in the tomb, you have sanctified the graves of the saints. By his glorious resurrection, you have brought life and immortality to light. In this hour, I pray, receive our thanks for that victory over death and the grace which he has obtained for us and for all who sleep in him. Keep us in everlasting fellowship with all who wait for you and in union with him who is the resurrection and the life, who lives and reigns with you and the Holy Spirit, ever one God, world without end. Amen.

Then the minister may pronounce one of the following benedictions:

May the God of peace, who through the blood of the eternal covenant brought back from the dead our Lord Jesus, that great Shepherd of the sheep, equip you with everything good for doing his will, and may he work in us what is pleasing to him, through Jesus Christ, to whom be glory for ever and ever. Amen.

The grace of our Lord Jesus Christ and the love of God and the fellowship of the Holy Spirit be with you all. Amen.

Section V
Special Church Occasions

Ordination of a Minister

The Meaning and Purpose of Ordination

Ordination for Christian ministry marks the completion of preliminary and preparatory steps for a person and a progression beyond licensure. It testifies to equipment for effective ministry. It reflects the concurrence of the minister and the body affirming the gift-mix of the servant, continuity in ministry, and a level of maturity achieved.

Ordination to Christian ministry, then, is a celebration of the reality of God's gift to the body in the person of a special minister (apostle, prophet, evangelist, pastor-teacher) who is endowed, qualified, and ready to equip the body for their work of ministry. It is the affirmation of the church of these things present in an individual, confirmed in assignment to a specific task.

A Service of Ordination

Prelude

Call to Worship

How, then, can they call on the one they have not believed in? And how can they believe in the one of whom they have not heard? And how can they hear without someone preaching to them? And how can they preach unless they are sent? As it is written, "How beautiful are the feet of those who bring good news!"

(Romans 10:14-15)

Invocation

Hymn

(continued on next page)

Scripture Lesson or Responsive Reading
> *Leader:* There are different kinds of gifts,
> *People: But the same Spirit gives them.*
> *Leader:* There are different kinds of service.
> *People: But the same Lord is served.*
> *Leader:* There are different kinds of working.
> *People: But the same God works all of them in all men.*
> *Leader:* Now to each one the manifestation of the Spirit is given for the common good.
> *People: All of these are the work of one and the same Spirit, and he gives them to each one, just as he determines.*
> *Leader:* Now you are the body of Christ.
> *People: And each one of you is a part of it.*
>   1 Corinthians 13:4-7, 11, 27)

Prayer

Hymn or Special Music

Ordination Sermon

Rite of Ordination

Hymn

Benediction

Rite of Ordination

Presentation
> *When the ordination sermon has been preached, an official of the church board (or an ordained minister or other appropriate person) comes forward with the person to be ordained and presents the candidate (and spouse) with the following words:*

Bishop _____, speaking for the people of this church, I present _____ to be ordained for Christian ministry, (along with his/her spouse who stands with him/her in this work).

Examination by the Bishop

_____, for some time now you have served God and the church in Christian ministry. You have completed a course of study. You have satisfied the Board for Ministry and Doctrine that you are sound in faith and fit to minister the Word. You have had the support of this congregation as you moved toward this day. You are acquainted with this body and its beliefs, and you are aware of the work to which you have been called.

As you come to this moment of ordination, I call upon you to answer the following questions that we may discern your readiness for this step:

Do you trust in Jesus Christ as your Savior and acknowledge him to be Lord of the world and head of the Church?

Answer: I do

Do you believe the Scriptures of the Old and New Testaments to be the inspired Word of God, and that they are the unique witness to Jesus Christ and God's authoritative word for your faith, life, and ministry?

Answer: I do.

Do you receive and endorse our church's teachings and practices as faithful to the principles of Holy Scripture?

Answer: I do

Do you accept the government and polity of our church, and are you willing to be guided thereby?

Answer: I am

Do you assume the responsibility to preach and teach God's Word with love and boldness; to minister to the needs of your people without partiality; and to build up the body of Christ?

Answer: God helping me, I do.

Will you be diligent in prayer and in the study of the Scriptures; and will you seek to model the Christian life among the people whom you serve?

Answer: God helping me, I will.

Will you seek to be directed and empowered of the Holy Spirit in order that you may be a faithful minister before the Lord among this people?

Answer: I will.

(To the minister's spouse):
_____, as you stand here with _____, do you declare your support of him/her and the ministry to which he/she is called; and do you purpose to walk together with him/her as he/she ministers, laboring with him/her as you have opportunity and gifts?

Answer: I do.

Prayer of Ordination
The candidate and spouse will kneel, and the bishop will lay his hands upon them and pray the prayer of ordination. If appropriate, other ordained ministers present may be invited to come forward and join with the laying on of hands.

Words of Ordination
The candidate (and spouse) will stand and the bishop will say:
In the name of the Lord and by the authority of the Brethren in Christ Church, I commit to you the responsibilities and privileges of ordination to Christian ministry and declare you duly ordained as a minister of the gospel of Christ. Take to yourself this ministry in the name of the Father, and of the Son, and of the Holy Spirit. Amen.

The bishop will then greet the newly ordained minister.

Charge to the Newly Ordained Minister
By the bishop or another minister.

Consecration of General Church Officers

At the meeting of the General Conference where General Church Officers are selected, the chairperson of the Executive Committee of the Board of Administration will preside in the consecration of these persons.

At the appropriate time the chairperson of the Executive Committee will state the officers elected, share the duties of the offices, and proceed with the service of installation as follows:

My dear colleagues, you have been called by the General Conference of the Brethren in Christ Church in North America to serve as General Officers in the positions of _____ for the period of _____. At this time you assume the responsibilities of your office(s). We pray that you may be enabled to faithfully perform your duties in the fear of God. May you be kept in humble harmony with Christ, the Head of the Church. May you be strengthened for your labors by the presence and power of the Holy Spirit within.

I now confer upon you your respective offices of the General Conference of the Brethren in Christ Church with all the rights and obligations pertaining thereto, in the name of the Father, and of the Son, and of the Holy Spirit.

Prayer of consecration with the laying on of hands.

The chairperson greets each officer with a handshake signaling the entrusting and acceptance of office.

Consecration of Bishops

The service of consecration of bishops will ordinarily take place during General Conference under the direction of the General Church Officers. The minister in charge will be appointed by that body. The bishops to be consecrated will occupy the front seats in the auditorium. After an appropriate opening the service of consecration will proceed as follows:

The Consecration Charge
The bishops to be consecrated will stand before the official in charge.

Minister in Charge: My brothers, before you are admitted to this ministry, hear this charge from the Scriptures and from the church which has called you:

The Brethren in Christ Church has expressed confidence in you—your character, your devotion to Christ and his cause, and your ability to direct and promote the general affairs and interests of the entire church. To this end you have been called to this significant responsibility by your brothers and sisters.

The Apostle Paul presents the qualifications of a bishop as follows: "An overseer must be above reproach, . . . temperate, self-controlled, respectable, hospitable, able to teach. . . . He must also have a good reputation with outsiders, so that he will not fall into disgrace and into the devil's trap."

The church which called you has assigned to you the following duties as bishop:

To model a life of spiritual maturity with competence in the areas of relationship, discernment, time usage, and encouragement.

To serve as counselor for pastors and families by building trust, by being a careful listener, and through mutual sharing.

To equip pastors for ministry by encouraging them in planning, goal setting, and leadership development.

To stimulate congregations by your preaching and to facilitate the selection of pastoral leadership.

To administer the regional conference in the development of a strategy for congregational health, evangelism, and church planting.

To share the denomination's vision and mission so that a spirit of unity will be present among the several congregations.

Examination

Minister in Charge: My brothers, the Scriptures command that we should not be hasty in admitting any person to governance in the Church of Christ. Therefore, before you receive this ministry, I call upon you to answer these questions in the fear of the Lord, that all here may know your mind and purpose concerning this sacred office.

Are you persuaded that you are called to this ministry by the church in accordance with the will of our Lord Jesus Christ?

Answer (each candidate individually): I am.

Will you endeavor to live soberly, righteously, and godly as a bishop in the church, so that you may be an example to all others in Christian living?

Answer: I will, by the help of God.

Will you instruct those under your care from the Word of God unto the edification of the whole church?

Answer: I will do so, the Lord being my helper.

Will you give diligence to faithfully perform the duties assigned you as a bishop in the Church of Christ, according to the order and direction of the Brethren in Christ Church?

Answer: I will, by the help of God.

Within your ability to do so, will you maintain and set forward quietness, love, and peace among all people, dealing justly and kindly with those in ministry and with all others over whom you have responsibility?

Answer: I will do so, by the grace of God, the Holy Spirit being my helper.

Prayer of Consecration

The conference body will now be asked to rise as prayers of consecration are offered in the following way: The official in charge will select persons in advance to represent each of the several conferences. The representatives will identify with the bishop-elect for the conference with which they are associated. In an order determined by the presiding official, the representatives will place hands upon the bishop-elect and will offer a prayer of consecration.

Response of the Conference

Minister in Charge: Do you, my brothers and sisters, under God accept these men as your appointed leaders, and will you give them your ready cooperation and support as they seek to carry out their responsibilities?

Response of delegates: We will do so, God being our help.

Installation

Minister in Charge: In the name of our Lord Jesus Christ, the Head of the Church, and by the authority vested in me by this General Conference, I hereby install each of you as bishop of the Brethren in Christ Church.

Benediction

The Lord bless you and keep you: the Lord make his face shine upon you and be gracious unto you; the Lord lift up his countenance upon you and give you peace. Amen.

Hymn *(Suggested hymn: "Pour Out Thy Spirit From On High")*

Consecration of a Deacon

Deacons, after being elected by the congregation, are installed in their office by consecration at the beginning of each term of service. The service of consecration may be a part of any duly called service of the congregation. The bishop will be notified of plans to consecrate a deacon and informed of the completion of this service. The pastor conducts the consecration.

Preparation

The service of consecration may include an appropriate sermon setting forth the responsibilities of all Christians to be servants and dealing specifically with the responsibilities and ministry of those called to the Office of Deacon. A part of the preparation is the reading of Acts 6:1-10 and 1 Timothy 3:8-13.

The minister will then address the congregation as follows:
Brothers and sisters in the Lord: God, through the Holy Spirit, has directed the church from its early days to the present time to set apart called people to look after its temporal interests and to labor for the spiritual unity and growth of the members of Christ's body. Learning from the New Testament, we call these servants deacons. Persons called to this service express loyalty to God by their service to the church. They are spiritually minded and possess wisdom and discernment in dealing with the affairs of the church. The _____(Name of Congregation)_____ Church, having full confidence in the faithfulness, loyalty, wisdom, and spiritual integrity of Brother _____ and/or Sister _____, according to the practice of our fellowship, have called him/her/them to the office of deacon.

Prayer

The minister then leads the congregation in prayer.

(continued on next page)

Examination

The persons to be consecrated now come forward and stand before the minister.

Minister: Forasmuch as the church has called you to assume the office of deacon, I now request that you answer the following questions:

Do you declare anew your faith in the gospel of our Lord Jesus Christ and your allegiance to him and his Church?

Candidate: I do.

Minister: Do you purpose to fervently cultivate your spiritual life by Bible reading, prayer, and Christian witnessing?

Candidate: I do.

Minister: Do you purpose to encourage and lead the church in deepening spiritual life and in her ministries of compassion?

Candidate: I do.

Minister: Do you purpose to further the interests of this church to the best of your ability, and to cooperate with the pastor and members in promoting the harmonious and effective working of the whole?

Candidate: I do.

Minister: Do you then accept the office of deacon in this body of Christ, and promise to faithfully perform its duties?

Candidate: I do, the Lord being my helper.

Minister (to the spouse when applicable):
The call of _____(Deacon's name)_____ is a call to you as well. Do you consent to the call of this congregation upon your husband/wife to serve as deacon, and will you walk with him/her in this ministry as you have opportunity and God gives you grace?

Spouse: Yes.

Prayer of Consecration

In the minister's own words or as follows:

Eternal God, you have given your Spirit to human beings that they may have power for temporal and spiritual service. You have sent your Son not to be served but to serve. Now we set apart and consecrate these your servants to the office of deacon, that they may serve in your name. Grant them deep compassion for all human needs; fill them with tender care and steadfast love for every person for whom Christ died. Inspire them with devotion to your church. Grant them growth in faith, that they may lead others by precept and example. Grant to the church grace to work with them for the nurture and the peace of your family. Sustain them through all their labors until their earthly work is done and they are fully with you in your kingdom. Through Jesus Christ our Lord. Amen.

Charge

The minister will then say: In the name of our Lord Jesus Christ, you are now set apart in the office of deacon to serve the Lord and the people of the _____ congregation. May you experience God's special grace in this calling.

Response of the congregation

We, the members of this body of Christ, in the spirit of joy, and in renewed loyalty to our Lord, acknowledge and receive you as deacon(s) and promise to pray for and support you in confidence, encouragement, cooperation, and prayers, that together we may increase in the knowledge and the love of God, manifest to us in Jesus Christ our Lord. Amen.

Commissioning of a Missionary

The consecration of a missionary may be performed at a service especially planned for the occasion, or it may be a part of a regular worship service. In the latter case only the ritual sections of the service will be used. The service is usually conducted by the pastor of the congregation.

Hymn

Call to Worship

Leader: I tell you, open your eyes and look at the fields! They are ripe for harvest.

Congregation: *Even now the reaper draws his wages, even now he harvests the crop for eternal life.*

Leader: The harvest is plentiful, but the workers are few.

Congregation: *Ask the Lord of the harvest, therefore, to send out workers into his harvest field.*

Invocation (in the words of the leader)

Introduction

Some of Jesus' final words on earth were: " . . . Go and make disciples of all nations, baptizing them in the name of the Father and of the Son and of the Holy Spirit, and teaching them to obey everything I have commanded you."

In response to that call, we have met here today in the name of the Lord to consecrate these before us who have heard the call of God to serve as missionaries and who are under appointment of the church through its agencies to fulfill this commission.

Scripture Lesson

One of these suggested passages: Psalm 67; 96; Isaiah 42:1-9; John 17:20-26; Acts 13:1-4; 14:21-28; 20:22-35; Ephesians 3:1-13.

Hymn

Prayer

Offering

Special Music

Sermon

Hymn

Ritual of Consecration

Presentation by a person designated by the Board for World Missions or other agency:

Representing the _____(Agency name)_____, I present to you Brother and Sister _____ (or "these candidates") who have been duly appointed as missionaries of the Brethren in Christ Church.

They have been found qualified for such service. We now present them to be consecrated to the service to which they have been called and appointed.

The missionaries will now stand before the minister officiating.

Declaration

Leader: You have heard the Great Commission which Christ gave to his first disciples. You believe that this commission applies to all followers of Christ today, and that it is incumbent upon them, insofar as may be possible, to devote their lives to the extension of his kingdom on earth. Specifically, you have come to sense the call of God upon *you* to respond to this high calling summoning you to this work. You have found this call confirmed by the circumstances of your life and the call of the church. You have been appointed to serve as missionaries, and having accepted the appointment, you are now to be consecrated to this high and holy service.

Charge to the Missionaries

We rejoice with you that in the providence of God, a door of service has been opened for you in the work of the Church of Jesus Christ. You are accorded a special opportunity and challenge in this set-apart ministry of teaching, preaching, and healing. Such service confers a great privilege, but it also is one which lays upon you a solemn responsibility. The personal consecration of your life to God for service is here made a public act in the presence of this congregation.

Examination of the Missionaries

Question: Have you sensed within yourself a deep love for people and a strong passion for their salvation, and have you felt clearly called of God to missionary service?

Answer: I truly believe I have.

Question: Do you give yourself unreservedly to the work of Christ in the area to which you are assigned, relying on God's grace; and do you make it your purpose to walk with Christ as his servant, faithful in word and deed, and in hearty cooperation with your fellow workers?

Answer: I do.

Question: Will you submit to leadership, be loyal to the church, and walk humbly with God in the work to which he has called you?

Answer: With his help, I will.

Missionaries now kneel. (Other missionaries and former missionaries may be invited to join the candidates at the front for the prayer of consecration.)

Prayer of Consecration

There will be a general prayer of consecration by the leader or appointee for all here being recognized. Following the prayer of consecration, the leader will take the hand of each person being commissioned and, stating the name, will say:

_____, I commission you to take the gospel of our Lord Jesus Christ into all the world, in the name of the Father, and of the Son, and of the Holy Spirit. Amen.

When all have been commissioned, the leader will conclude by saying:

Go, in the assurance that the One who called you has also promised to go with you, even to the end of the age.

Benediction *(in the leader's own words, or as follows):*

The peace of God, which transcends all understanding, will guard your hearts and minds in Christ Jesus. May the blessing of God Almighty, the Father, the Son, and the Holy Spirit, be upon you, and remain with you always. Amen.

Installation of a Pastor

The service of installation for a pastor should be conducted during a Sunday morning worship service if at all possible. A bishop or his appointee will officiate. The rite of installation is a part of a worship service such as the following:

Prelude

Call to Worship

Invocation and the Lord's Prayer

Hymn

Scripture Lesson
  Suggested Selections: Numbers 27:15-23; Romans 10:1-15; Ephesians 4:1-16; 2 Timothy 4:1-8.

Prayer

Hymn

Sermon

Special Music

Announcement of Installation
  Bishop: The coming of _____ to the pastoral ministry of this congregation marks a new step in the life of this body. We believe the appointment of_____ has been ordained of God and it is therefore proper for both the congregation and the pastor to receive and give pledges of their consecration to the upbuilding of God's cause and kingdom here.

Charge to the Congregation

Bishop: Having called this man of God to be your minister, do you now solemnly pledge to him your prayerful interest, your sympathetic understanding, and your faithful support?

Congregation: We do.

Bishop: Do you promise to attentively hear his preaching of the Word, to participate reverently in the services of worship, to share with him in the responsibilities of teaching and learning, to assume your proportionate part of the church's benevolent ministries, to receive him into your hearts and homes, to counsel with him concerning the welfare of the church and winning of souls, to encourage him in his stand for the right, to forgive him when he makes mistakes, and to follow his leadership as he follows Christ?

Congregation: We do.

Charge to the Pastor and Spouse

Bishop (addressing the pastor): Having been invited to be the pastor of this congregation, do you take this people to be your people, this field of labor to be your field as the call of God for this time?

Pastor: I do.

Bishop: Do you promise to give yourself faithfully to the ministry of the Word and to prayer, to be a good shepherd to this flock of God, to minister to the needs of all alike, to be the friend of all who will permit you, to seek the salvation of souls and the nurture of the saved, and to put the service of Christ and his kingdom above all else?

Pastor: I do, with God's help.

Bishop: Do you promise that if you are wronged, you will forgive as you expect to be forgiven, to seek always to keep yourself mentally alert and physically fit, as much as lies within you to be at peace with all men, and to lead this congregation in the ways of Christ as the Holy Spirit may give you wisdom and power?

Pastor: I do, with God's help.

Bishop (addressing the pastor's spouse): _____, do you join in this pledge by declaring before God and this congregation your willingness to support your husband/wife, to cooperate with him/her in this ministry, and in every way possible to assist in building the kingdom of God in this pastorate?

Pastor's spouse: I do.

Prayer of Installation *(by the bishop)*

Declaration of Installation

Bishop: Since you have been called to this ministry by the Pastoral Committee of the congregation and the General Conference Pastoral Stationing Committee, I declare you, _____, to be the pastor of _____ Church, and I pray that God's richest blessings may attend your ministry and leadership in this congregation, in the name of the Father, and of the Son, and of the Holy Spirit. _____, these are your people.

The newly-installed pastor responds with personal words and concludes the service with a benediction or in another appropriate manner.

Installation of Other Members of the Ministry Team

A service of presentation and installation is appropriate in cases when a congregation calls assistant or auxiliary ministers to the congregation. This may take place under the leadership of the pastor during a regular worship service of the church, with the following ritual inserted at an appropriate place in the service. This one ritual may readily be adapted for various ministry positions in the church, such as Assistant or Associate Minister, Minister of Music, Minister of Christian Education, Minister of Visitation, or Minister of Administration. Insert the appropriate terms at points indicated.

Introduction

Pastor: As pastor of this congregation, it is my joy and privilege to present to you _____(Name of person)_____, who has been called to serve as _____(Title)_____ for this church. He/she has met the approval of the Church Board and myself as being of one faith and purpose with us; therefore, he/she has been invited to join our staff in ministry here. It is appropriate that we share in a formal installation as we come to this moment.

Pledge

Pastor (addressing the team member): My dear brother/sister in Christ, in entering upon this work, do you faithfully promise that by the help of God, you will endeavor to perform the duties appointed for you in the ministry of this church?

Team member: I do.

Pastor (addressing the congregation): Do you, the people of this church, receive _____(Name of person)_____ as _____(Title)_____ here, and do you promise to support him/her in ministry among us? If so, indicate your purpose by standing.

Installation

Pastor (addressing the team member): In the name of the Lord Jesus Christ, the Head of the Church, we welcome you as the _____(Title)_____ in this congregation. May the blessing of God the Father, the Son, and the Holy Spirit, rest upon you and abide with you always.

Prayer *(in the words of the pastor, or as follows):*

Lord, God of the Church, who blesses the body with servants to equip the members for the work of ministry: we pray your special blessing and supply of grace upon this your servant as he/she undertakes this ministry among us. As we commend this one to you, we pray you would give him/her a devout, faithful, and willing spirit. May your servant be enabled to guide and direct your church, to the salvation of sinners and the edification of believers in the holy faith. Amen.

Benediction

The Lord bless you and keep you; the Lord make his face shine upon you and be gracious unto you; the Lord turn his face toward you and give you peace. Through Jesus Christ our Lord. Amen.

Installation of Sunday School Officers and Teachers

This order of installation may be used during a regular Sunday school session, in a Sunday morning worship service when Christian education is the theme of the day, or at any other appropriate time.

Hymn

As the hymn is being sung, the officers and teachers of the church school to be installed will come to stand before the minister.

Charge

Minister: Friends and co-workers: We are gathered here in the presence of God to recognize those who have responded to his call to the work of teaching and administration in the church school. In calling you to be teachers and officers here, the church has committed to you as important a task as any within her reach to bestow. Yours is the high privilege of guiding and inspiring boys and girls, men and women in the ways of Jesus Christ, our Lord. In this you are co-laborers together with God. By your words and example you will be constantly influencing those entrusted to your care.

I charge you, therefore, to be faithful, earnest, sympathetic, and persevering, keeping ever in mind that the great end of Christian education is not merely the imparting of information, but also the awakening and inspiring of the spirit. As Jesus increased in wisdom and stature and in favor with God and man, so may your pupils grow in grace and in the knowledge of God.

Here the Minister of Christian Education or the chairperson of the Board of Christian Education may read the names of the officers and teachers of the Sunday school.

Covenant of Teachers and Officers

Minister: Inasmuch as you have been called to the ministry of teaching and leading in Christian education in this church, will you endeavor with God's help to discharge your duties faithfully? Will you be diligent in study; regular and punctual in attendance at Sunday school and church; and will you maintain a sympathetic and friendly contact with your pupils, earnestly seeking by word and example to win them to Jesus Christ and the church?

Teachers and Officers: We will.

Pledge of the Members of the Sunday School

The minister may then address the members of the Sunday school as follows:

As the teachers and officers have presented themselves to God in consecration to their various tasks, it is proper that we as members of this congregation should dedicate ourselves to the same work, and that we should publicly assume our obligation to support them by our loyalty and prayers. I call you, then, as members in the Sunday school of this church to join me in this commitment.

Will you show your appreciation and cooperation for these leaders by determining to do your part, to be regular in attendance, attentive in interest, true to the ideals of the church school, and loyal to the Master whom we serve? If so, stand with me.

(Congregation stands for prayer.)

Prayer of Consecration *(in the minister's own words or as follows):*

Eternal God and our Father, you have called us into your service and have promised us grace and strength for fulfilling your will. Look with favor upon your servants who now dedicate themselves to their tasks in this church. Fill them with wisdom and insight, that they may discern the latent possibilities in the lives of those they teach. May they never grow weary in their efforts to win to Christ those for whom they have responsibility. Fill each with your Spirit, and grant that they may realize that in all their efforts you are their companion, their leader, and their

117

friend. Bless the parents and help them to show forth in their lives and in their homes the influences that will strengthen their children to stand firm under the pressures of life. Give to those who teach and to those who are taught the spirit of understanding and obedience. May they increase in wisdom and stature, and in favor with God and man. In the name of Jesus, our master teacher, we pray. Amen.

Hymn

Benediction

Now to him who is able to do immeasurably more than all we ask or imagine, according to his power that is at work within us; to him be glory in the church and in Christ Jesus throughout all generations, for ever and ever! Amen.

Installation of Officers of Youth Organizations

The youth of the church may be recognized by the planning of a Sunday evening service such as the following. In this, or a service appropriately adapted, the officers of the youth organization of the congregation are installed.

Prelude

Call to Worship
Seek the Lord while he may be found; call on him while he is near.

Invocation
O God, our Father, in the worship of this hour we seek your presence. Upon all that we do we ask your blessing. Unto you we dedicate our prayers, our hymns, our very thoughts, in the name of our Lord Jesus Christ. Amen.

Hymn

Scripture

Prayer

Music *(by members of the youth organization)*

Responsive Reading
Leader:	Blessed are they whose ways are blameless, who walk according to the law of the Lord.
Congregation:	*Blessed are they who keep his statutes and seek him with all their heart.*
Leader:	They do nothing wrong; they walk in his ways.

(continued on next page)

Congregation:	*You have laid down precepts* *that are to be fully obeyed.*
Leader:	Oh, that my ways were steadfast in obeying your decrees!
Congregation:	*Then I would not be put to shame* *when I consider all your commands.*
Leader:	I will praise you with an upright heart as I learn your righteous laws.
Congregation:	*I will obey your decrees;* *do not utterly forsake me.*
Leader:	How can a young man keep his way pure? By living according to your Word.
Congregation:	*I seek you with all my heart;* *do not let me stray from your commands.*
Leader:	I have hidden your word in my heart that I might not sin against you.
Congregation:	*Praise be to you, O Lord;* *teach me your decrees.*
Leader:	With my lips I recount all the laws that come from your mouth.
Congregation:	*I rejoice in following your statutes* *as one rejoices in great riches.*
Leader:	I meditate on your precepts and consider your ways.
Congregation:	*I delight in your decrees;* *I will not neglect your word.*

(Psalm 119:1-16)

Hymn

Offering

Hymn

Installation Rite

The officers will now stand before the officiating minister.

Minister: God, by his Holy Spirit, calls people to serve him according to the gifts bestowed upon them. You have been called by God and your friends to serve the youth group by God's help. Will you accept the office to which you have been chosen?

Answer: I will.

Minister: In accepting this office, will you promise to faithfully perform all its duties to the best of your ability?

Answer: I will, the Lord being my helper.

Minister: As an officer of the youth group, will you promote the cause of Christ and the church, helping to meet the spiritual and social needs of the members of the youth group?

Answer: I promise to do so.

Minister (addressing the members of the organization): And now, will you as members of the youth organization acknowledge and receive these officers? Will you promise to cooperate and work with them according to the word of God, so that God's cause may be advanced?

Answer: We will.

Prayer *(in the minister's own words or as follows):*
We ask you, Lord, to set apart these officers as they begin the work of leading the youth group. Give them wisdom, we pray, and grace, that they may serve this group well. Fill them with your Holy Spirit and faith as they administer their offices in the fear of the Lord. May the ministry of the youth group increase and advance because of your blessing and their diligence. Equip each one for their respective duties and enable them to be faithful in all things. Through Jesus Christ our Lord, Amen.

Installation
It is my privilege to install you as officers of the __(Youth group name)__ in the name of the Father, and of the Son, and of the Holy Spirit. Amen.

Sermon

Hymn

Benediction
The Lord bless you and keep you: the Lord make his face shine upon you and be gracious unto you; the Lord turn his face toward you and give you peace.

Dedication of a Church Building

The dedication service presented here includes an entire order of worship and ritual. This may be used in place of a regular service of the church, as a special service of dedication, or the ritual may be used as a part of a regular worship service.

Prelude

Call to Worship
    Leader: I will praise you, O Lord, with all my heart:
                       I will tell of all your wonders.
    Congregation: *I will be glad and rejoice in you; I will sing*
                       praise to your name, O Most High.

Hymn

Scripture Lesson
    Suggested Passages: 2 Chronicles 6:12-15, 40-42; Psalm 15; 24; 84; Isaiah 6:1-8, or a responsive reading, such as Psalm 84.

Prayer

Hymn or Anthem

Dedication Address

Hymn or Anthem

Recognitions and Appreciation

Presentation of the Key
    The chairman of the Building Committee will say to the pastor:
    The Building Committee has completed the work assigned to it by the congregation. Therefore, as chairman of the Building

Committee, I present to you the key of the church *(giving key to the pastor).*

The pastor in turn addresses the bishop or the officiating minister who will dedicate the building and will say:
The Building Committee appointed to supervise the erection of this church has completed its work and now presents to you the key of the building *(give the key to the bishop)* and requests you to dedicate it to the work and glory of God.

Dedication *(by the bishop or officiating minister):*
Since God in mercy has prompted his people to build this place of worship and service for his glory and the good of his people and has prospered its construction, let us now set it apart for these purposes in dedication to the Almighty.

To the eternal God our Father, maker of heaven and earth, author and giver of life, who in the person of Jesus Christ his Son has made known to us the power of his redeeming love, and who by his gracious Holy Spirit is ever seeking to bring light out of darkness,

Congregation: We dedicate this house of worship.

Leader: For the preaching of the Word of God that brings hope to the discouraged, comfort to those who mourn, healing to the afflicted, strength to the tempted, and salvation to all people,

Congregation: We dedicate this house of worship.

Leader: For the promotion and support of Christian missions and the relief of suffering among people near and far by our prayers and financial gifts,

Congregation: We dedicate this house of worship.

Leader: For the experience of the unity of the Spirit which transcends our diversities and makes us one in Christ Jesus, our glorious head,

Congregation: We dedicate this house of worship.

(continued on next page)

Leader: In remembrance of all those who have gone before us and those who have sacrificed to make the completion of this building a reality,

Congregation: We dedicate this house of worship.

Leader: For the singing of his praises, for meditation upon God's Word, for communion in his presence and for fellowship with his people,

Congregation: We dedicate this house of worship in all its parts and furnishings to the glory of God.

Leader and Congregation: That it may be to all people a house of prayer, a haven of comfort, a community of fellowship, and a gate to heaven, we dedicate this house of worship.

Prayer of Dedication *(in the leader's own words or as follows):*
Lord God of the Church, your people have built this house for your worship and glory. You are above all the heavens and you fill the immensity of the universe with your greatness. Nevertheless, we pray that you will accept this offering in the name of your Son, our Savior. You saw fit to dwell in the temple of old; now, wherever two or three are gathered in your name, you are among them. May this house of worship be preserved from all unholy purposes and activities. May it be devoted to your service alone to the redemption and upbuilding of mankind, through Jesus Christ. Amen.

Dedication Offering

Hymn

Benediction
Now to him who is able to do immeasurably more than all we ask or imagine, according to his power that is at work within us, to him be glory in the church and in Christ Jesus throughout all generations, for ever and ever! Amen.

Dedication Litany
(An alternative to the ritual suggested above.)

Leader: In this moment of dedication of this building for worship, it is appropriate that we come in reverence before the Lord our God. The Most High does not dwell in temples made with hands. Yet he commanded Moses to prepare a tabernacle and allowed Solomon to build a temple, and blessed both with the evidence of his presence and glory. Our Lord has assured us that he will meet with his people where but two or three gather in his name. We are assured, then, that God will accept this house which we have built for his glory and purposes. Having this confidence, we now dedicate this facility unto the Triune God— Father, Son, and Holy Spirit—to be his sanctuary where his Word is preached, the ordinances administered, and services conducted to his glory.

To these ends we also dedicate ourselves to him with all that we are and possess, to be his through the covenant of grace by Jesus Christ our Lord.

The Act of Dedication
The people will stand and join in the responses.

Leader: We set apart this house to the worship of the living and true God, and to the service of Jesus Christ our Lord.

Congregation: We devote it to the preaching of the gospel of the grace of God for the conversion of sinners, and to the education of Christians in the knowledge of spiritual wisdom in all the activities of the Christian life.

Leader: Here shall prayer and praise ascend to God. Here shall the ordinances of the Lord's house be observed.

Congregation: Here shall the Word of God be proclaimed for the salvation of the lost and a perpetual light to guide God's people in the ways of life.

Leader: Here may sinners find release and Christians find support and strength in the rigors of life.

(continued on next page)

Congregation: May no discordant note of strife be heard within these walls, no unholy spirit of pride or worldliness find entrance.

Leader: May God graciously accept this offering of a building in his name—an offering made by grateful hearts and willing hands—and bless every person that shares in this gift.

Congregation: May many here be born of God, so that when all these here today shall have gone to their eternal home, others will take up the service until Jesus comes.

Leader: To the glory of God our Father, by whose favor we have built; to the honor of Jesus the Christ, the Son of the living God and our Savior; to the praise of the Holy Spirit, source of life and light,

Congregation: We dedicate this house.

Leader: To the sanctification of the family; to the training and nurture of childhood; to the inspiration of youth and the salvation of all,

Congregation: We dedicate this house.

Leader: To the help of the needy; to the promotion of Christian community; to the extension of God's rule through the whole world,

Congregation: We dedicate this house.

Dedication Prayer

Transfer of Keys
The leader will now ask the chairman of the Board of Trustees to come forward and will say to him:
The Building Committee of this church has completed its work. Therefore, by this act of transfer of the keys, the members of the Building Committee commit to you, the trustees of this church, the responsibility of the care of this building.

I charge you as chairperson of the Trustee Board with the responsibility given by the General Conference of the Brethren in Christ Church: "The Trustees shall adequately insure, care for and keep in necessary repair all church property. In no case shall they be privileged to expend money for extensive repairs or alterations without the consent of the group(s) whom they serve."

As you accept this key, do you accept the accompanying responsibilities?

Response: We do.

Continue the dedication service with the offering, hymn, and benediction as outlined above.

Dedication of a Baptistry

The following ritual is suggested for inclusion in a regular Sunday morning worship service. It may be incorporated either before or following the sermon.

Responsive Reading
All or parts of the reading may be included.

Minister: Then Jesus came from Galilee to the Jordan to be baptized by John.

Congregation: But John tried to deter him, saying, "I need to be baptized by you, and do you come to me?"

Minister: Jesus replied, "Let it be so now; it is proper for us to do this to fulfill all righteousness." Then John consented.

Congregation: As soon as Jesus was baptized, he went up out of the water. At that moment heaven was opened, and he saw the Spirit of God descending like a dove and lighting on him.

Minister: And a voice from heaven said, "This is my Son, whom I love; with him I am well pleased."

Congregation: Then Jesus came to them and said, "All authority in heaven and earth has been given to me."

Minister: "Therefore go and make disciples of all nations, baptizing them in the name of the Father and of the Son and of the Holy Spirit,

Congregation: "Teaching them to obey everything I have commanded you. And surely I will be with you always, to the very end of the age."

Minister: When the people heard this, they were cut to the heart and said to Peter and the other apostles, "Brothers, what shall we do?"

Congregation: Peter replied, "Repent and be baptized, every one of you, in the name of Jesus Christ so that your sins may be forgiven. And you will be forgiven. And you will receive the gift of the Holy Spirit."

Minister: What shall we say, then? Shall we go on sinning so that grace may increase?

Congregation: By no means! We died to sin; how can we live in it any longer?

Minister: Or don't you know that all of us who were baptized into Christ Jesus were baptized into his death?

Congregation: We were therefore buried with him through baptism into death in order that, just as Christ was raised from the dead through the glory of the Father, we too may live a new life.

Minister: If we have been united with him in his death, we will certainly also be united with him in his resurrection.

Congregation: For we know that our old self was crucified with him so that the body of sin might be rendered powerless, that we should no longer be slaves to sin—because anyone who has died has been freed from sin.

Minister: Now if we died with Christ, we believe that we will also live with him.

Congregation: For we know that since Christ was raised from the dead, he cannot die again; death no longer has mastery over him.

Minister: The death he died, he died to sin once for all; but the life he lives, he lives to God.

Congregation: In the same way, count yourselves dead to sin but alive to God in Christ Jesus.

The Act of Dedication

Minister: Christ has left with us his example and injunction concerning baptism. This powerful ordinance which he instituted is filled with rich symbolism, deep significance, and special meaning. In this act of obedience the Christian symbolizes participation in the burial and resurrection of our Lord and finds in that experience the joy of witnessing to identification with Christ in the new life of the Spirit. Today we dedicate this baptistry in the _____ Church to its sacred use as a place where persons may make their witness to faith in Christ and, as he did, they may "fulfill all righteousness."

To the recognition of Christ as the author of eternal salvation; to the confession of faith in his power to make people whole; to the renunciation of sin and the acceptance of the abundant life assured through him;

Congregation: We dedicate this baptistry.

Minister: To the consecration of those who, having long walked without him, now declare their purpose to turn and serve him; to the dedication of youth with their promise to serve Christ faithfully; and to the reconsecration of all who shall here witness the observance of this holy ordinance;

Congregation: We dedicate this baptistry in the name of God the Father, the Son, and the Holy Spirit. Amen.

Prayer of Dedication

The worship service continues in its assigned order following the completion of the prayer of dedication.

Dedication of a
Christian Education Facility

This is a suggested ritual for the incorporation of a dedication service within a regular order of worship. If an entire service of dedication is desired, the order for a dedication of a church may be adapted for this use.

Call to Worship
Leader: Worship the Lord in the splendor of his holiness; tremble before him, all the earth.
Congregation: God is spirit, and his worshipers must worship in spirit and in truth.

Declaration of Purpose
Leader: This building, which in the providence of God and the labor of people has been completed, declares our vision and purpose for the Christian education of the children, youth, and adults of the congregation. For this task we need not only the best that people can do, but above all the blessing of Almighty God, the source of wisdom and knowledge. We bring, therefore, our thanks and praises for his aid in this undertaking, and we offer our prayers on behalf of those who give themselves and their gifts in fulfilling the purposes for which this facility has been prepared.

Hymn

Scripture
Suggested passages: Psalm 119:9-16; Proverbs 3:13-18; Matthew 7:24-27.

Responsive Reading
Leader: Wisdom has built her house;
she has hewn out its seven pillars.
Congregation: Does not wisdom call out?
Does not understanding raise her voice?

(continued on next page)

Leader: On the heights along the way,
    where the paths meet, she takes her stand;
*Congregation: Beside the gates leading into the city,
    at the entrances, she cries aloud:*
Leader: "To you, O men, I call out;
    I raise my voice to all mankind."
*Congregation: "You who are simple, gain prudence;
    you who are foolish, gain understanding."*
Leader: "Listen, for I have worthy things to say;
    I open my lips to speak what is right.
*Congregation: "My mouth speaks what is true,
    for my lips detest wickedness.*
Leader: "Choose my instruction instead of silver,
    knowledge rather than choice gold,"
*Congregation: "for wisdom is more precious than rubies,
    and nothing you desire can compare with her."*
Leader: But where can wisdom be found?
    Where does understanding dwell?
*Congregation: The fear of the Lord—that is wisdom,
    and to shun evil is understanding.*

Rite of Dedication

The trustees or appropriate committee will come forward to deliver the keys to the leader, and one of them will say:

We present this building to be dedicated to the glory of God and for his service in the instruction and nurture of people in Christian faith.

Minister (with the congregation standing): Buildings erected for service in the name of our Lord and Savior Jesus Christ should be formally and devoutly set apart for their special uses. We would not only dedicate this building, but also the gifts and services of those who labored in its planning and construction. Furthermore, we would dedicate the labors of those who will serve in the tasks of Christian education for which this facility is constructed.

Now, therefore, we give ourselves anew to the service of God: our labor, that it may be according to God's holy will; our bodies, that they may be fit temples for the indwelling of the Holy Spirit; our spirits, that they may be renewed after the image of Christ.

In the name of God—the Father, the Son, and the Holy Spirit—we dedicate this building to the holy ministry of Christian education.
Let all the people say:

Congregation: Amen.

Leader: We dedicate this building to the continual search for abundant life that is in Christ, both for each individual and for the world. May all that is done within these walls be to the honor and glory of God in unfolding human life. Let all the people say:

Congregation: Amen.

Prayer *(in the minister's own words or the following):*
God of grace and mercy, at all times guide the thoughts and labors of your people to the end that your purposes will be fulfilled in their lives. Grant us all to know that which is worth knowing, to love that which is worth loving, to praise that which pleases you most. Grant us true judgment to distinguish truth from error, courage to disdain all that is evil, and strength to do all those things that we know to be right in your sight; through Jesus Christ our Lord. Amen.

Benediction
To him who is able to keep you from falling and to present you before his glorious presence without fault and with great joy—to the only God our Savior be glory, majesty, power and authority, through Jesus Christ our Lord, before all ages, now and forevermore! Amen.

Dedication of a Church Organ

This ritual is planned for use within an order of worship. When used separately, appropriate Scriptures, prayers, and acts of worship should be added.

Presentation
The minister will call forward the person designated to present the instrument (the donor or appointee, chairman of the procurement committee, or minister of music) who will say:

We present this organ to be dedicated to the glory of Almighty God and for the service of this church.

Responsive Reading
It is good to praise the Lord
and make music to your name, O Most High,
to proclaim your love in the morning
and your faithfulness at night,
to the music of the ten-stringed lyre
and the melody of the harp.
for you make me glad by your deeds, O Lord;
I sing for joy at the works of your hands.

Gloria Patri

Dedicatory Music
Dedicatory music will be played on the instrument being dedicated.

Act of Dedication
Minister: David was the father of the service of song in public worship. He was not only a poet and sweet singer, but he also instituted the use of instruments of music to lead the songs of worshipers. The use of instruments has continued to this day. Today the organ is an appropriate instrument of music for use in Christian worship. Responding to dedicated hands, the organ can aid in inspiring the heart in worship. Let us now dedicate this

instrument, whose music we have heard, to the ministry of music in God's house.

To the exaltation and worship of God through melodies of praise and gratitude;

Congregation: We dedicate this organ.

Minister: To summon his people to the hour of worship and praise, and to sound the call to God's encompassing love;

Congregation: We dedicate this organ.

Minister: To lift our spirits to communion with Christ, to stir our hearts to seek higher levels of holy living, and to bring to our lives the comfort, peace and hope which abide in Christ;

Congregation: We dedicate this organ in the name of God: the Father, the Son, and the Holy Spirit. Amen.

Prayer of Dedication *(in the words of the minister or as follows):*
Our Father, whom the generations have worshiped in harmonies of sweet sound, be pleased to accept this instrument as a means of praising you. Grant that its music may be a blessed benediction upon all who worship here. Assure to all musicians who shall sound its notes, and to all worshipers who shall be lifted Godward by its voice, that there may come at times the sweep of hallelujahs from the heavenly hosts, and the whispers of your voice from your eternal grace. Amen.
Therefore with angels and archangels, and with all the company of heaven, we laud and magnify your glorious name, evermore praising you and saying:

Congregation (saying or singing):
Holy, holy, holy, Lord God of hosts:
Heaven and earth are full of thy glory!
Glory be to thee,
O Lord most high! Amen.

Benediction

Dedication of a Parsonage

This service is a modification of the dedication of a Christian home. It usually is conducted as a worship service on Sunday or Wednesday evening under the direction of the bishop or pastor.

Opening Remarks
Peace be to this house. Except the Lord build the house, they labor in vain that build it.

Home was the first institution created of God for his children. The home is the cradle of faith and of education, the foundation of government and civilization. We are here to invoke divine blessing upon the home for the minister of our church, that the ties of love in this home may be strong and beautiful through the blessing and inspiration of the heavenly Father, and that whoever lives in this home may be an example and a testimony to this congregation and this community for our Lord Jesus Christ.

The Doxology

Prayer (by the minister in charge. This may be closed with the following verse):
O Thou whose gracious presence blessed
The home in Bethany;
This shelter from the world's unrest,
This home made ready for its guest,
We dedicate to Thee.

We build an altar here, and pray
That thou wilt show Thy face.
Dear Lord, if Thou wilt come to stay,
This home we consecrate today,
Will be a holy place. Amen.

Louis F. Benson

Scripture Lesson

Dedication Ritual

Leader: Who presents this parsonage to be dedicated to God and his service?

The trustees or their representative stand and one says:
We present to you this house to be dedicated to the service of almighty God through its use as a dwelling place for the minister of our church and his family. We now present to you this key which locks and unlocks the doors of this house. Along with our giving you the key, we pledge our willingness to keep this house for its appointed use.

Charge to the Trustees

Leader: You who have been chosen to serve as trustees of this parsonage are called to act in behalf of the church in exercising oversight of this property.

We trust you to keep it in good repair so that it will present an attractive and inviting appearance, that its silent influence in the community may contribute to the glory of God.

Act of Dedication

(If the pastor is leading the service, the following may be said by a trustee or deacon on behalf of the congregation):

We herewith give ourselves and our gifts as we dedicate this building to the holy ministry of sheltering the family that sustains such a singular relationship to this congregation and community. May this home fulfill a vital role in creating good fellowship among the members of this congregation, and may those who abide here conduct the affairs of the congregation wisely.

We, therefore, in the name of God: the Father, Son, and Holy Spirit, dedicate this building as the parsonage of the _____ Brethren in Christ Church.

Prayer *(in the leader's own words, or as follows):*

Lord God, our heavenly Father, Giver of life, we pray that you will make this home an abode of light and love. Grant that all that is pure, tender, and true may grow up under its shelter. Let all that hinders godly living and sound relations be driven far from it.

(continued on next page)

Make it the center of refreshing and holy influence. May those who enter here sense the sweet presence of your grace and be blessed.

Let your work appear unto your servants, and your glory unto their children. Let the beauty of the Lord our God be upon us, and establish the work of our hands upon us. The praise shall be yours forever. Amen.

Special Music

The singing of "Bless This House" by a group or individual may appropriately be included.

Benediction

The Lord bless you and keep you; the Lord make his face shine upon you and be gracious unto you; the Lord turn his face toward you and give you peace. Amen.

Dedication of a Home

A practice of significance and great potential value is the dedication of a house which is to be the dwelling place for a family. This may be a parsonage or any house which a family wishes to dedicate to God for his glory as a haven for his children. The ritual presented here is for a service of such dedication.

This service may be held in the living room of the house—before the fireplace if the house has one. Four unlighted candles may be placed on a table near the fireplace. A plate of bread and a pitcher of fruit juice may be placed beside the candles.

The minister who conducts the service will take a place at the left of the table facing the fireplace (if used). The family (and guests, if any) will stand beside the minister facing in the same direction.

The service may be opened by a suitable hymn or chorus, a selection from the piano, or a number on another musical instrument.

Minister: Peace be to this house. Except the Lord build the house, they labor in vain that build it.

Home was the first institution created of God for his children. Home is the cradle of religion, of education, of government, and of civilization. We are here to pray God's blessing upon this home, that its ties of love may be strong and beautiful through the blessing and inspiration of the heavenly Father.

The Doxology *(sung by all present)*

Prayer *(by the minister. He may close his prayer with the following verse):*

O Thou whose gracious presence blessed
The home in Bethany;
This shelter from the world's unrest,

(continued on next page)

This home made ready for its guest,
We dedicate to Thee.
We build an altar here, and pray
That thou wilt show Thy face.
Dear Lord, if Thou wilt come to stay,
This home we consecrate today,
Will be a holy place. Amen.

Louis F. Benson

Scripture

The minister or another person may read selections or all of the following:

Hear, O Israel: The Lord our God, the Lord is one. Love the Lord your God with all your heart and with all your soul and with all your strength. These commandments that I give you today are to be upon your hearts. Impress them on your children. Talk about them when you sit at home and when you walk along the road, when you lie down and when you get up. Tie them as symbols on your hands and bind them on your foreheads. Write them on the doorframes of your houses and on your gates.

(Deuteronomy 6:4-9)

As Jesus and his disciples were on their way, he came to a village where a woman named Martha opened her home to him. She had a sister called Mary, who sat at the Lord's feet listening to what he said. But Martha was distracted by all the preparation that had to be made. She came and asked, "Lord, don't you care that my sister has left me to do the work myself? Tell her to help me!"

Martha, Martha," the Lord answered, "you are worried and upset about many things, but only one thing is needed. Mary has chosen what is better, and it will not be taken away from her."

(Luke 10:38-42)

For this reason I kneel before the Father, from whom his whole family in heaven and on earth derives its name. I pray that out of his glorious riches he may strengthen you with power through his Spirit in your inner being, so that Christ may dwell in your hearts through faith. And I pray that you, being rooted and established in love, may have power, together with all the saints, to grasp how wide and long and high and deep is the love of

Christ, and to know this love that surpasses knowledge—that you may be filled to the measure of all the fullness of God.

Now to him who is able to do immeasurably more than all we ask or imagine, according to his power that is at work within us, to him be glory in the church and in Christ Jesus throughout all generations, for ever and ever! Amen.

(Ephesians 3:14-21)

Dedication

The husband, wife, and children (if any) who are to occupy this home read the following dedicatory lines as indicated.

Husband: To you, O God, you who live with the humble to shield them with your strong arm of protection, guide them with your Spirit, and order their way;

Family (light the first candle and say together): We dedicate this home and light the candle of devotion.

Wife: As a house of friendship and caring where others may come for fellowship, neighboring, and sociability, to share their thoughts, needs, burdens, and aspirations, and be enabled to go forth strengthened in body, mind, and spirit;

Family (light the second candle and say together): We dedicate this home and light the candle of friendship.

Husband: To beauty in art and literature, where pictures and books shall be friends, and music and song the language of comfort and inspiration;

Family (light the third candle and say together): We dedicate this home and light the candle of beauty.

Wife: To the Great Guest, Jesus Christ our Lord, who broke bread with those who loved him, and who brought the light of heaven and the peace of God to people like ourselves;

Family (light the fourth candle and say together): We dedicate this home and light the candle of service, and we break bread together as a token of hospitality. *(Break the bread and pour the drink and share it with everyone present.)*

Prayer (by the minister, in his own words or as follows):

O God, our heavenly Father, whose Son, our Lord, by his presence blessed the home in Bethany: Bless, we pray, this home, that your love may rest upon it, and that your promised presence may be manifest in it. May all the members of this household grow in grace and in the knowledge of you and of our Lord and Savior Jesus Christ. Teach them to love one another as you commanded us; and help us all to choose that better part which will not be taken away from us; through Jesus Christ our Lord. Amen.

Hymn

Benediction

The Lord bless you and keep you; the Lord make his face shine upon you and be gracious unto you; the Lord turn his face toward you and give you peace. Amen.

A Groundbreaking Service

A service of groundbreaking is a fitting act for a people at the location where the construction of a new facility is planned. The members of the congregation as well as the leaders of the community and friends of the church may be invited to share the occasion.

The service is generally conducted following a morning worship service.

Call to Worship

Great is the Lord, and most worthy of praise,
in the city of our God, his holy mountain.
Enter his gates with thanksgiving
and his courts with praise;
give thanks to him and praise his name.

Invocation

Scripture *(Suggested portion: Matthew 7:24-27)*

Prayer

Remarks

The Scriptures clearly declare that unless the Lord build the house, they labor in vain who build. The Psalmist declared,
How lovely is your dwelling place,
O Lord Almighty!
My soul yearns, even faints
for the courts of the Lord;
my heart and my flesh cry out
for the living God.

(continued on next page)

We rejoice together in the prospect of breaking ground for a building to be constructed on this site to the glory of God. Our hope is that this spot may indeed be holy ground where many may find the presence and manifestation of the Lord precious to their lives. May this occasion help us to break up the fallow ground of our hearts, knowing it is time to seek the Lord.

We pray and trust that this act may symbolize for us the planting of the good seed of the kingdom in good soil, looking toward a bountiful harvest. As we plan to build, may we be continually reminded that we are laborers together with God in work to which he calls us.

Whereas, we are constituted as a people of God, believers in Jesus Christ who is our Savior and Lord, and conscious of his commissioning us to be his witnesses, we therefore proceed to take this first step in this building program of the _____ Church.

Let us now proceed to turn this soil (sod) on which we stand, that here may be erected a temple to his praise, a permanent witness to the people, a house of worship, and a place for spiritual nourishment and inspiration as we grow together in Christ.

At this time our respected brother/sister, _____, having received this shovel from the hand of our contractor, _____, and _____, our architect, will take shovel in hand and turn a piece of soil (sod).

The soil is turned. Following this, other selected persons may turn over one or more shovelsful of earth as a part of the ceremony.

Now that we have taken the first step toward the erection of this building, may there be a prayer on all our hearts that the blessings of God may attend our progress in the completion of this building. May God bring us all with the finished structure to the day of dedication of it, together with ourselves, to the honor and glory of his holy name.

Hymn

Benediction

A Service for Laying a Cornerstone

This service is planned as a special service of worship. If it is to be incorporated as part of a regular worship service, some of the elements of worship will be omitted.

Call to Worship
> Our help is in the name of the Lord,
> the Maker of heaven and earth.
> Unless the Lord builds the house,
> its builders labor in vain.

Doxology

Scripture
> *Suggested passages: Psalm 24; 46; 96; 100*

Prayer

Hymn (by the congregation or a designated group)

Remarks or Meditation
> *Suggested texts: 1 Chronicles 28:20; 29:16; Psalm 127:1; Ephesians 2:20; 1 Peter 2:6*

Minister: Dear brothers and sisters, we have gathered here to lay the cornerstone of a new house for the worship of almighty God. We come in confidence that he looks with favor upon this purpose as we devoutly seek his blessing on this undertaking.

Prayer (in the minister's own words or as follows):
Almighty and everlasting God: You are ever exalted and yet always near. Grant that we may worthily offer unto you—the Father, Son, and Holy Spirit—this foundation which is laid for the building of a church. Let this be a place where your glory will be manifest among us and where the people will call upon your name. Let your blessing rest upon those who labor in building

this house; shield them from all harm, and grant them and all of us here present your heavenly grace that our gifts and service may be sanctified unto your purposes. Amen.

Laying of the Cornerstone
The minister will exhibit a box to be deposited and announce its contents. This box may contain such articles as a Bible, a church hymnal, church periodicals, programs, brochures, photos, names of pastors who have served the congregation, membership lists, and other documents and artifacts that will have relevance.

The minister, assisted by the builder, will deposit the box in the stone, place mortar, then striking the stone will say:

In the name of God, the Father, the Son, and the Holy Spirit, we lay this cornerstone of a house to be built and dedicated to the worship and service of almighty God.

Gloria Patri

Benediction

146

Mortgage or Note Burning

This ceremony is appropriate as a part of a Sunday morning worship service. The minister may preach a sermon on the subject of Christian stewardship. Or the occasion may be a special service dedicated to the purpose indicated. Such a service may well include something of the history of the congregation, high points in the life of the church, and expressions from persons associated with the church across the years.

At the point in the service when the mortgage is to be burned, the trustees are invited to appear before the minister. In lieu of the actual mortgage, a facsimile may be used for burning in the ceremony.

Minister: The earth is the Lord's, and everything in it,
the world, and all who live in it;
for he founded it upon the seas
and established it upon the waters.

People: *Who may ascend the hill of the Lord?*
Who may stand in his holy place?
He who has clean hands and a pure heart,
who does not lift up his soul to an idol
or swear by what is false.
He will receive blessing from the Lord
and vindication from God his Savior.
Such is the generation of those who seek him,
who seek your face, O God of Jacob.

Prayer

Remarks by the Historian

The historian will offer a brief historical statement regarding the beginnings of the church and of the present facility. These should include information about the past indebtedness and its clearance.

147

Remarks by the Chairperson of the Board of Trustees

Under the blessing of God we have arrived at this hour. Through the dedication and sacrifice of these people, the last dollar of indebtedness on this building has been paid. Now we present to you, the pastor of this church, the mortgage to be burned. *(Hands the mortgage to the pastor.)* This is a day of victory and achievement. Let us give thanks to God and rejoice in it.

Response by the Pastor

We thank God today and rejoice together that we have arrived at this place of victory and blessing. Through the dedication and liberality of the people of this congregation, the debt on this facility has been paid. I believe that your faithfulness, loyalty, and generosity are pleasing to our heavenly Father. This church is an expression of your love to God. With gratitude and thankfulness we give praise to him.

Today's celebration is a milestone: it marks the beginning of a larger service for this church as we walk together in faithfulness and dedication. As we burn this mortgage, a symbol of labor and devotion in the past, we light a flame to the future in commitment to continue our service and labors for God in this place.

The minister lights a candle and passes it to the appointed person who ignites the mortgage. As this takes place, the minister says the following:

Pastor: Jesus said, "I am the light of the world. Whoever follows me will never walk in darkness, but will have the light of life." Furthermore, he said, "You are the light of the world. A city on a hill cannot be hidden. Let your light shine before men, that they may see your good deeds and praise your Father in heaven." Let us devote ourselves anew to the task begun here long ago.

Doxology *(sung by the congregation as the mortgage is burning)*

Benediction

Section VI
Special Times and Seasons

As humans we are given to times and seasons. Six days of labor and the seventh of rest. Winter, spring, summer, fall. Plowing, planting, growing, harvest, storing. Passover, Pentecost, Atonement, Tabernacles. These are a part of our experience. For some, the times and seasons have become organized into law and ritual; for others they are of little importance. As non-liturgical people, we have not come to mark the seasons with precision and to name every Sunday. Still, there is some value in noting that very early in its history, the church marked times and seasons. Each Lord's Day was an observance of the resurrection. This became the focal point around which Christian days and seasons developed. If the development has become too elaborate for some, the concept yet speaks to the human situation and deserves some attention in a minister's manual.

Special Days of the Christian Year

Days of the Christian Calendar

The first half of the Church Year: Advent through Pentecost (Sunday nearest November 30 through the seventh Sunday after Easter)—*God speaking to humanity through revelation.*

ADVENT—Anticipating the coming of the Word
  Advent Sunday, or First Sunday in Advent—Sunday nearest November 30, followed by the Second, Third, and Fourth Sundays in Advent.
CHRISTMASTIDE—The Word made flesh
  Christmas—December 25 through January 6, Epiphany Eve
EPIPHANY SEASON—The Word manifest
LENT—The response of the believer in self-examination and renewal
  Ash Wednesday through Easter Eve—The 40 days before Easter (Sundays excluded)
HOLY WEEK—Palm Sunday through Easter Eve
  Maundy Thursday—the night of the Lord's Supper
  Good Friday—the day of the crucifixion
EASTER
PENTECOST SUNDAY—The Church is born

The second half of the Church Year: Pentecost to Advent— *Humanity responding to God through commitment.*

151

Using the Christian Year

In strict liturgical churches, every Sunday is given a name and has Scripture lessons designated for the Sunday. Services revolve around the events. In non-liturgical churches, the minister is free to decide the topics and content of the service. This can be liberating—or a burden. Are some times more appropriate for some emphases than others? The Christian year can be a guide around which to build the themes and topics for the year. It may help the minister avoid hobbying on a few themes at the expense of the whole gospel. It may provide direction when it seems difficult to discern the mind of the Spirit for the time. Certainly, the use of the Christian year in planning one's work must be as servant and not as master.

Materials for the Seasons

Abundant materials are available for the major days of the Christian year—Christmas and Easter. Materials are more sparse for the less commonly observed times and seasons. Sources such as the *Book of Common Prayer* of the Protestant Episcopal Church (earlier edition) and *The Worshipbook* of the Joint Committee on Worship of the Presbyterian Churches provide Scripture readings, collects, and prayers for the several days.

Other Special Days

A great temptation confronts the minister to observe every national holiday and popular "special day" of the calendar. Use of such days to develop themes and build services has both dangers and values: Mother's Day, Father's Day, Memorial Day, Independence Day (U.S.), Canada Day, and Labor Day are not a part of the Christian year as such. To incorporate them into the flow of the Christian year may cause confusion among worshipers who do not make clear distinctions in such matters. On another hand, there are emphases to be made that can utilize such days to good advantage. Mother's Day or Father's Day present good opportunities to deal with the Christian home; Labor Day to consider the Christian and work; and Independence Day or Canada Day to treat the subject of the Christian and nation-states. The minister must let Christian truth and the Scriptures be the guidelines while avoiding faddishness.

Section VII
Aids and Reference

Creeds

The Apostles' Creed

I believe in God the Father Almighty, maker of heaven and earth;

And in Jesus Christ his only Son our Lord; who was conceived by the Holy Ghost, born of the Virgin Mary, suffered under Pontius Pilate, was crucified, dead, and buried. He descended into hell; the third day he arose again from the dead. He ascended into heaven, and sitteth on the right hand of God the Father Almighty; from thence he shall come to judge the quick and the dead.

I believe in the Holy Ghost; the holy catholic church; the communion of saints; the forgiveness of sins; the resurrection of the body; and the life everlasting. Amen.

The Nicene Creed

I believe in one God the Father Almighty, maker of heaven and earth, and of all things visible and invisible;

And in one Lord Jesus Christ, the only-begotten Son of God; begotten of his Father before all worlds; God of God, Light of Light, very God of very God; begotten, not made, being of one substance with the Father; by whom all things were made; who for us men and for our salvation came down from heaven, and was incarnate by the Holy Ghost of the Virgin Mary, and was made man, and was crucified also for us under Pontius Pilate. He suffered and was buried, and the third day he rose again according to the Scriptures, and ascended into heaven, and sitteth on the right hand of the Father. And he shall come again, with glory, to judge both the quick and the dead; whose kingdom shall have no end.

And I believe in the Holy Ghost, the Lord, and Giver of Life, who proceedeth from the Father and the Son; who with the Father and the Son together is worshiped and glorified; who spoke by the prophets. And I believe in one catholic and apostolic church. I acknowledge one baptism for the remission of sins, and I look for the resurrection of the dead, and the life of the world to come. Amen.

Calls to Worship

Morning

Hear, O Israel: The Lord our God, the Lord is one. Love the Lord your God with all your heart and with all your soul and with all your strength.

Deuteronomy 6:4-5

Who may ascend the hill of the Lord?
    Who may stand in his holy place?
He who has clean hands and a pure heart,
    who does not lift up his soul to an idol
    or swear by what is false.

Psalm 24:3-4

Wait for the Lord;
    be strong and take heart
    and wait for the Lord.

Psalm 27:14

Glorify the Lord with me;
    let us exalt his name together. . . .
Great is the Lord, and most worthy of praise . .

Psalm 34:3; 48:1

Be still, and know that I am God;
I will be exalted among the nations,
I will be exalted in the earth.

Psalm 46:10

How lovely is your dwelling place,
    O Lord Almighty!
My soul yearns, even faints
    for the courts of the Lord;
my heart and my flesh cry out
    for the living God.

Psalm 84:1-2

I will sing of the Lord's great love forever;
    with my mouth I will make your faithfulness
    known through all generations.
        Psalm 89:1

It is good to praise the Lord
    and make music to your name, O Most High,
to proclaim your love in the morning
    and your faithfulness at night . . .
        Psalm 92:1-2

Shout for joy to the Lord, all the earth. . . .
Enter his gates with thanksgiving
    and his courts with praise;
    give thanks to him and praise his name.
For the Lord is good and his love endures forever;
    his faithfulness continues through all generations.
        Psalm 100:1, 4-5

Give thanks to the Lord, for he is good;
    his love endures forever.
Let the redeemed of the Lord say this—
    those he redeemed from the hand of the foe . . .
        Psalm 107:1-2

O give thanks to the Lord, for he is good;
    his love endures forever.
This is the day the Lord has made;
    let us rejoice and be glad in it.
        Psalm 118:1, 24

I lift up my eyes to the hills—
    where does my help come from?
My help comes from the Lord,
    the Maker of heaven and earth.
        Psalm 121:1-2

I rejoiced with those who said to me,
    "Let us go to the house of the Lord."
        Psalm 122:1

Seek the Lord while he may be found;
  call on him while he is near.
Let the wicked forsake his way
  and the evil man his thoughts.
Let him turn to the Lord, and he will have mercy on him,
  and to our God, for he will freely pardon.
Isaiah 55:6-7

The Lord is in his holy temple;
  let all the earth be silent before him.
Habakkuk 2:20

Your Father knows what you need before you ask him.
. . . Seek first his kingdom and his righteousness, and all these
things will be given to you as well.
Matthew 6:8b, 33

Come to me, all you who are weary and burdened, and I will
give you rest. Take my yoke upon you and learn from me, for I
am gentle and humble in heart, and you will find rest for your
souls. For my yoke is easy and my burden is light.
Matthew 11:28-30

Yet a time is coming and has now come when the true
worshipers will worship the Father in spirit and truth, for they are
the kind of worshipers the Father seeks. God is spirit, and his
worshipers must worship in spirit and in truth.
John 4:23-24

Come near to God and he will come near to you. Wash your
hands, you sinners, and purify your hearts, you double-minded.
James 4:8

Responses
Come, let us bow down in worship,
  let us kneel before the Lord our Maker;
For he is our God
  and we are the people of his pasture,
  the flock under his care.
Psalm 95:6-7

Sing to the Lord a new song;
    sing to the Lord, all the earth.
Sing to the Lord, praise his name;
    proclaim his salvation day after day.
Declare his glory among the nations,
    his marvelous deeds among all peoples.
For great is the Lord and most worthy of praise.
    Psalm 96:1-4a

Praise the Lord, O my soul;
    all my inmost being, praise his holy name.
Praise the Lord, O my soul,
    and forget not all his benefits.
    Psalm 103:1-2

Praise the Lord, all you nations;
    extol him, all you peoples.
For great is his love toward us,
    and the faithfulness of the Lord endures forever.
Praise the Lord!
    Psalm 117

Give thanks to the Lord, for he is good.
    His love endures forever.
Give thanks to the God of gods.
    His love endures forever.
Give thanks to the Lord of lords.
    His love endures forever.
    Psalm 136:1-3

Evening

It is good to praise the Lord
    and make music to your name, O Most High,
to proclaim your love in the morning
    and your faithfulness at night . . .
    Psalm 92:1-2

O Lord, I call to you; come quickly to me.
> Hear my voice when I call to you.
May my prayer be set before you like incense,
> may the lifting up of my hands be like the evening
> sacrifice.
>> *Psalm 141:1-2*

On the evening of that first day of the week, when the disciples were together, with the doors locked for fear of the Jews, Jesus came and stood among them and said, "Peace be with you!"
> *John 20:19*

Advent and Christmas

A voice of one calling:
> "In the desert prepare the way for the Lord;
make straight in the wilderness
> a highway for our God. . . .
The glory of the Lord will be revealed,
> and all mankind together will see it.
>> For the mouth of the Lord has spoken."
>> *Isaiah 40:3-5*

Arise, shine, for your light has come,
> and the glory of the Lord rises upon you. . . .
Nations will come to your light,
> and kings to the brightness of your dawn.
>> *Isaiah 60:1, 3*

"She will give birth to a son, and you are to give him the name Jesus, because he will save his people from their sins."

All this took place to fulfill what the Lord had said through the prophet: "The virgin will be with child and will give birth to a son, and they will call him Immanuel"—which means, "God with us."
> *Matthew 1:21-23*

Do not be afraid. I bring you good news of great joy that will be for all the people. Today in the town of David a Savior has been born to you; he is Christ the Lord.
> *Luke 2:10b-11*

Suddenly a great company of the heavenly host appeared with the angel, praising God and saying,
"Glory to God in the highest,
and on earth peace to men on whom his favor rests."
Luke 2:13-14

The Word became flesh and lived for a while among us. We have seen his glory, the glory of the one and only Son, who came from the Father, full of grace and truth.
John 1:14

Epiphany and New Year

. . . Your years go on through all generations.
In the beginning you laid the foundations of the earth,
and the heavens are the work of your hands.
They will perish, but you remain;
they will all wear out like a garment. . . .
But you remain the same,
and your years will never end.
Psalm 102:24b-27

The Spirit of the Sovereign Lord is on me,
because the Lord has anointed me
to preach good news to the poor.
He has sent me to bind up the brokenhearted,
to proclaim freedom for the captives
and release for the prisoners,
to proclaim the year of the Lord's favor . . .
Isaiah 61:1-2a

He who was seated on the throne said, "I am making everything new! . . . I am the Alpha and the Omega, the Beginning and the End . . . He who overcomes will inherit all this, and I will be his God and he will be my son."
Revelation 21:5-7

Pre-Easter/Lent

Create in me a pure heart, O God,
    and renew a steadfast spirit within me.
Do not cast me from your presence
    or take your Holy Spirit from me.
The sacrifices of God are a broken spirit;
    a broken and contrite heart,
    O God, you will not despise.
          Psalm 51:10-11, 17

Because of the Lord's great love we are not consumed,
    for his compassions never fail.
They are new every morning;
    great is your faithfulness.
          Lamentations 3:22-23

"Even now," declares the Lord,
    "return to me with all your heart,
    with fasting and weeping and mourning."
Rend your heart
    and not your garments.
Return to the Lord your God,
    for he is gracious and compassionate,
slow to anger and abounding in love . . .
          Joel 2:12-13

If we walk in the light, as he is in the light, we have fellowship with one another, and the blood of Jesus, his Son, purifies us from all sin.
If we confess our sins, he is faithful and just and will forgive us our sins and purify us from all unrighteousness.
          1 John 1:7, 9

Palm Sunday

Lift up your head, O you gates;
    lift them up, you ancient doors,
    that the King of glory may come in.
Who is he, this King of glory?
    The Lord Almighty—
    he is the King of glory.
          Psalm 24:9-10

The crowds that went ahead of him and those that followed shouted,

"Hosanna to the Son of David!"
"Blessed is he who comes in the name of the Lord!"
"Hosanna in the highest!"
Matthew 21:9

For God so loved the world that he gave his one and only Son, that whoever believes in him shall not perish but have eternal life. For God did not send his Son into the world to condemn the world, but to save the world through him.
John 3:16-17

Easter

The angel said to the women, "Do not be afraid, for I know that you are looking for Jesus, who was crucified. He is not here; he has risen, just as he said. Come and see the place where he lay. Then go quickly and tell his disciples: 'He has risen from the dead . . .' "
Matthew 28:5-7

Christ has indeed been raised from the dead, the firstfruits of those who have fallen asleep. . . . Listen, I tell you a mystery: We will not all sleep, but we will all be changed—in a flash, in the twinkling of an eye, at the last trumpet. For the trumpet will sound, the dead will be raised imperishable, and we will be changed.
1 Corinthians 15:20, 51

Thanksgiving Day

Give thanks to the Lord, call on his name;
    make known among the nations what he has done.
Sing to him, sing praise to him;
    tell of all his wonderful acts.
Glory in his holy name;
    let the hearts of those who seek the Lord rejoice.
1 Chronicles 16:8-10

May the peoples praise you, O God;
>may all the peoples praise you.
May the nations be glad and sing for joy,
>for you rule the peoples justly
>and guide the nations of the earth. . . .
Then the land will yield its harvest,
>and God, our God, will bless us.
God will bless us,
>and all the ends of the earth will fear him.
>*Psalm 67:3-4, 6-7*

Shout for joy to the Lord, all the earth.
Serve the Lord with gladness;
>come before him with joyful songs.
Know that the Lord is God.
>It is he who made us, and we are his;
>we are his people, the sheep of his pasture.
Enter his gates with thanksgiving
>and his courts with praise;
>give thanks to him and praise his name.
For the Lord is good and his love endures forever;
>his faithfulness continues through all generations.
>*Psalm 100*

Praise the Lord, O my soul;
>all my inmost being, praise his holy name.
Praise the Lord, O my soul,
>and forget not all his benefits.
He forgives all my sins
>and heals all my diseases;
he redeems my life from the pit
>and crowns me with love and compassion.
>*Psalm 103:1-4*

Invocations

God be merciful unto us and bless us, and cause your face to shine upon us, so that your way may be known upon earth, your salvation among all nations. Let the people praise you, O God; let all the people praise you. God, even our own God, shall bless us. Amen.

"O God, you are my God,
    earnestly I seek you;
my soul thirsts for you,
    my body longs for you,
in a dry and weary land
    where there is no water." *(Psalm 63:1)*

Father, may these words of the psalmist be our expression as we are in your presence this day. May our sense of need for you be deep and intense. And then, may we be satisfied with your own self in, around, and beneath us all. Through Jesus Christ our Lord, Amen.

Most Holy Father, may the hush of your presence move us now to adoration, and may all voices be stilled that yours may be heard. To think of you, O God, is rest; to know you is eternal life; to see you is the end of all desire; and to serve you is perfect freedom and everlasting joy; therefore, O God, we come to you. Hear our prayer, through Jesus Christ our Lord. Amen.

Almighty God, who has given us grace at this time with one accord to make our common supplications unto you; and promised that when two or three are gathered together in your name you will grant their requests; fulfill now, O Lord, the desires and petitions of your servants, as may be most expedient for them, granting us in this world knowledge of your truth, and in the world to come life everlasting. Amen.
Chrysostom

O God, whom heaven and the heaven of heavens cannot contain, but who dwells with those who are of an humble and contrite heart, look in mercy upon us as we are gathered here in your house for worship. May your Holy Spirit reveal divine truth to our hearts. Captivate our wandering thoughts that we may worship you in spirit and in truth and go from this place in peace. In Jesus' name. Amen.

Almighty God, unto whom all hearts are open, all desires known, and from whom no secrets are hid; cleanse the thought of our hearts by the inspiration of your Holy Spirit, that we may perfectly love you, and worthily magnify your holy Name; through Christ our Lord. Amen.
                    Book of Common Prayer

Great God, in whom we live and move and have our being, we come to offer ourselves to you as living sacrifices—body and spirit, thought and intent, word and action. Transform us, we pray, by the renewing of our minds that we may know and do your will wholly. Through Jesus Christ our Lord. Amen.

Almighty God, of whom the whole family in heaven and on earth is named, we bless you for a fellowship which joins earth and heaven, and unites us with the worshiping faithful of ages past, who have found in Christ the true meaning of life. We bless you for a fellowship which at this moment of our awareness becomes world wide, and makes us one with men and women of every land and nation who know him as Savior and Lord. May we be worthy members of this glorious company.
                    Alfred T. DeGroot

Our Father, again, as ever before, breathe upon us the blessings which we need—even that spirit of enlightenment, and of faith, and of love by which we shall know that we are your children, and rise into communion with you. Help us to lay aside all those influences that depress us, and which give strength to our senses. Give us those inspirations by which we may discern the invisible and the spiritual. And may the services of the sanctuary, and all the offering of our hearts, our thoughts, and our fellowship today be acceptable to you. And look lovingly upon us, that we may have joy and rejoicing in you. We ask it for Christ's sake. Amen.
                    Henry Ward Beecher

Our heavenly Father, we come with thanksgiving that we have a high priest who is able to sympathize with our weaknesses in that he was tempted as we, yet without sin. And so we approach the throne of grace with confidence, that we may receive mercy and find grace to help us in our time of need. Amen.

Offertory Sentences and Prayers

S. Each of you must bring a gift in proportion to the way the Lord your God has blessed you.

Deuteronomy 16:17

P. Our Lord, may this gift truly represent our consecration to your service. As we are increasingly prospered, may we also share in your cause with liberality and true devotion. We ask your blessing upon us in the name of him, who though he was rich, yet for our sakes he became poor, that we through his poverty might become rich. Amen.

S. The earth is the Lord's, and everything in it,
    the world, and all who live in it.

Psalm 24:1

P. We give thee but thine own,
    Whate'r the gift may be:
All that we have is thine alone,
    A trust, O Lord, from Thee.

William W. How

S. Splendor and majesty are before him;
    strength and glory are in his sanctuary.
Ascribe to the Lord, O families of nations,
    ascribe to the Lord glory and strength. . . .
    bring an offering and come into his courts.

Psalm 96:6-8

P. Father, if we can but discern your wonder and glory a little, it will bring us to your altar with our offerings—of our possessions and of ourselves. Enhance our vision, I pray, that we may perceive your splendor and give appropriately. Amen.

S. Honor the Lord with your wealth,
with the firstfruits of all your crops;
then your barns will be filled to overflowing,
and your vats will brim over with new wine.
Proverbs 3:9

P. Gold and silver you have, O Lord, and cattle on a thousand hills; the earth is yours and the fullness thereof. As stewards of your mercies, we present this offering before you. May it indeed be acceptable to you, we pray in Jesus' name. Amen.

S. "Bring the whole tithe into the storehouse, that there may be food in my house. Test me in this," says the Lord Almighty, "and see if I will not throw open the floodgates of heaven and pour out so much blessing that you will not have room enough for it."
Malachi 3:10

P. Father of us all, you have taught us that there is generosity that leads to abundance and withholding that comes to poverty. Open our eyes—and hearts—that we may discern the blessing which accompanies giving what belongs to you, and that we may give joyously of what you entrust to us. Amen.

S. Do not store up for yourselves treasures on earth, where moth and rust destroy, and where thieves break in and steal. But store up for yourselves treasures in heaven, where moth and rust do not destroy, and where thieves do not break in and steal. For where your treasure is, there your heart will be also.
Matthew 6:19-21

P. Curb our material desires, O Lord, and give us the willingness as your disciples to assume a simpler standard of life, thus to release more wealth for advancing your Kingdom on earth. Indeed may our treasures be in heaven. Through Jesus Christ our Lord. Amen.

S. Jesus said, "Seek first his kingdom and his righteousness, and all these things will be given to you as well."

Matthew 6:33

P. O Lord, we hear the assuring words of Jesus that our Heavenly Father knows what we have need of. He feeds the birds and clothes the grass in splendor. May our trust in him bring deliverance from worry and fretting as we bring these gifts for Kingdom work. In Jesus' name, Amen.

S. St. Paul said, "In everything I did, I showed you that by this kind of hard work we must help the weak, remembering the words the Lord Jesus himself said: 'It is more blessed to give than to receive.' "

Acts 20:35

P. Lord Jesus, all you were—and are—teaches us that it is more blessed to give than to receive—not just in things and money, but also in love and serving and pouring out our lives for others. In giving this offering we want to give as you gave, Lord Jesus, without reservation—that others might have blessing and life. Amen.

S. On the first day of every week, each one of you should set aside a sum of money in keeping with his income.

1 Corinthians 16:2

P. O God, our Father, be pleased to accept this offering of our money, the symbol of our love and devotion; and give your servants grace so to use it that your name may be honored among men, and the happiness and prosperity of your church increased, through Jesus Christ our Lord. Amen.

Arthur Cleaves

S. Each man should give what he has decided in his heart to give, not reluctantly or under compulsion, for God loves a cheerful giver.

2 Corinthians 9:7

P. Our Father, help us to realize that it is more blessed to give than to receive. Bless us in the giving, not merely of these temporal gifts, but of ourselves to your service, through Jesus Christ our Lord. Amen.

The Pastoral Prayer

The time of the pastoral prayer is a special moment in the worship service when the pastor brings the members of the congregation into the presence of God and lifts the needs and concerns of the people in intercession before the Lord. Certainly the pastor is not the only person who prays publicly in the worship service. But the pastor stands uniquely as God's representative in care for the congregation at this moment. Thus the pastor dare not approach this moment without thought or speak glibly at such a time.

Associated with the time of the pastoral prayer, many congregations include a "prayer and share" time in their worship service when the individual members bring their concerns before the body. This can be a precious time in the life of the congregation if it is properly incorporated into the pastoral prayer. The pastor will want to exercise care to include expressed concerns thoughtfully and tastefully while maintaining control during this time.

The pastor needs to be aware of the elements of prayer in reflecting upon the pastoral prayer. The counsel of the Apostle Paul is helpful: "And pray in the Spirit on all occasions with all kinds of prayers and requests" (Ephesians 6:18a). The pastoral prayer will typically include at least the following elements: praise, adoration, and thanks; confession and petition; request and intercession; submission and promise. The pastor applies these to the life of the congregation in its immediate context and its broader mission in the world.

All prayer of the Christian is addressed to God in the name of Jesus and it is his hearing that we desire and need. This is true of the pastoral prayer as of any other. In this situation, however, the pastor is standing with the people, leading them in the prayer. Therefore it is necessary that they hear and understand so that they can join their hearts in the prayer.

The pastor should identify with the people in the pastoral prayer. The prayer begins with an appropriate address to God with invocation, adoration, and thanksgiving—including thanks for the abundant provisions of God's grace and the reality of our spiritual relationship with him. This is followed by confession of need and intercession. In the areas of petition and intercession, thought should be given beforehand. Certain general matters are included in the prayer, but care should be given that the same ones are not mentioned every Sunday and that some phrases are not repeated weekly in the form of cliches. Needs and conditions that directly affect the congregation should be prayed for without becoming tedious and trifling. Each member should feel included in the prayer. The pastoral prayer should cause the entire congregation to sense the presence of God in the service and make it easy for them to put their hand in the hand of God.

A Pastoral Prayer

Our Father in heaven, we are gathered together in Jesus' name to worship you. Prepare us, we pray, to worship you in Spirit and in truth. You are worthy of worship and praise and adoration, for you are the Lord, God of the universe. We have nothing to bring that makes us worthy of your love and grace, but you have opened the way to fullness of life here and in the world to come. We come then at your invitation, realizing that we are totally dependent upon you.

We thank and praise you, Father, for your great love poured out upon us. We see it in the world around us, in your blessings upon our lives, and especially in the gift of your Son, Jesus Christ. We praise you for the gift of salvation through his work on Calvary and its outworking in the lives of those who believe. We thank you for the Holy Spirit, the Comforter, who walks among us and leads us into all truth. We thank you for your Word which is a light to our pathway. Grant us ready minds and willing hearts to walk in full obedience to your truth.

May your kingdom come and your will be done through this church. May the gospel be preached faithfully, the sick be healed, and evil forces in our community, our homes, and our lives be cast out. Let us be a people who make a difference for God in the places where we live—in the work place, the school, the home.

Father, you know us all—where we are obedient and where we are less than obedient; where we are strong and where we are weak; and where we are a help or where we are a hindrance. We need not make any explanations to you about ourselves, for you know us through and through. Speak to us today, that each of us may make decisions and commitments to follow you more faithfully and effectively. Enable us to be a blessing to one another, that our lives will be enriched together as we fellowship in this church.

Thank you, Father, for your blessings through this church: the fellowship of your people, the fellowship of prayer, the praises of the people, and the testimonies of your working among us. For some of us, life has been difficult recently. We pray for those who are experiencing sickness and the hand of affliction; may your healing power and grace visit these. We pray for those who are going through difficult times and stresses in life. We remember those who have lost their way; lead them in the path of righteousness. We pray for loved ones and neighbors who have not yet come to know you as Lord and Savior; may your Spirit reach them through some of us.

Let your blessings be upon our families. May each of our homes be a place where Christ is the head, where couples find direction and joy in their relation to you and to each other, and where our children learn of Jesus and his love for them.

Bless, we pray, those who serve in places of authority. Equip them with wisdom to know right, and courage to do it in these difficult times. Let the gospel extend with power around the world, and keep the doors open for the Christian witness.

Let our time together today be an equipping for greater blessing and service. May we go from this place with enlarged vision, with fresh anointing, and with a dedication to walk faithfully in response to your will. Our prayer is in Jesus' name with thanksgiving. Amen.

Prayers For
Special Days and Seasons

Christmas

Most holy and righteous God, our Father: You have revealed the glory of your love in the face of Jesus Christ and have called us by him to the fellowship of sonship. As we remember his nativity, fill our hearts, we beseech you, with the gladness of this great redemption. We would join in the heavenly song of glory to God in the highest, on earth peace and good will toward men. Breathe into our hearts the spirit of Jesus that we may fully trust and obey, and be sent out to live among people in Christian love and care.

As the Wise Men of old bowed at the feet of the holy child, Jesus, may we bow in true humility and present our bodies a living sacrifice, which is our reasonable service. Let there be in us a new birth of faith and hope and wonder, and the charity that thinks no evil. Make us such as we never yet have been, joyous in service, trustful and triumphant, in the name of Jesus our Lord. Amen.

New Year

Almighty and eternal God, the same yesterday, today, and forever: Our lives wax old as does a garment, but you are ever the same, and your mercy does not change. In the midst of these confused and shifting scenes, help us to find in you the constant and unfailing friend in whom we may place our confidence and from whom we may receive wisdom and strength, not only for the days of this new year, but for all the days that are to come; through Jesus Christ our Lord. Amen.

James D. Morrison

Good Friday

O Lamb of God, who takes away the sin of the world, our hearts are bowed in reverence and humility before the wonder of your cross. You have borne our griefs and carried our sorrows.

With your stripes we are healed, and the Lord has laid on you the iniquity of us all. By your temptation and obedience, the betrayal and forsaking, the scourge and piercing crown, the cruel wounding of the nails, the taunts and burning thirst, the lingering anguish of the cross which you have willingly endured for our salvation, grant us your pardon and your peace. Through dying you have conquered death, and risen again that we may share your life forevermore. Let your glory shine among the trials of the earth. Quicken our faith and make our love effective for your service. Draw us to yourself in true repentance and unfeigned humility, and may our lives bear witness to your love through all our years. Amen.

Hymns for the Living Age

Easter

Almighty God, our Father, who is not the God of the dead but of the living, we give you joyful thanks this Easter morn for him who is the resurrection and the life. We believe in him, his life, his death, and his resurrection. Grant that in this sacred hour we may be aware of him, not as a far-off, blessed memory, but as our eternal Lord and Savior who was dead and is alive forevermore. By the power of his resurrection may people everywhere rise out of selfishness and sin into a divine fellowship with yourself. Lead us in our worshiping this day, and hear us as we pray the prayer he taught us saying, Our Father in heaven . . .

Adapted from James D. Morrison

Pentecost

O Lord our Lord, how excellent is your name in all the earth! You are God and beside you there is none other. You are eternally the same—a forgiving, compassionate, and merciful Father. You have never neglected nor forsaken your people. The works of your hands give witness of your glory and power. Through your holy child Jesus you have revealed to us a Savior by whom we have forgiveness of our sins. Through the shedding of his blood we also are cleansed from the defilement of the sin nature and made a vessel sanctified and fit for the Master's use.

We thank you for the present witness and presence of your Holy Spirit in our lives. According to your promise he is sent into the world to give birth to your body, the Church, whose inauguration we celebrate today. We thank you for the empowerment of your children who seek to be sanctified wholly and filled with the Holy Spirit. According to your Word, you work in us both to will and to do your good pleasure. We thank you, our Father, that through your Spirit we are enabled to live holy and blameless in this sinful world among whom we shine as lights.

Grant us, we pray, a fresh anointing of your Spirit today. Work in us the same boldness and power for witnessing as your disciples received at Pentecost. Help us to yield our wills in perfect harmony with your will for us. Prepare and bless your Church in the work of evangelizing the world. Continually cleanse and sanctify her through the washing of water by the Word. Make her ministers firebrands of truth. Destroy any indifference and lethargy among your people. By your Spirit select and prepare the bride for your Son Jesus, and keep her in constant and expectant readiness for his soon coming. With thanksgiving we call on you to hear our prayer, through Jesus Christ our Lord. Amen.

Mother's Day

Lord God our Father, you have poured out upon us in our earthly dwellings the blessings of heavenly places. You sanctified and blessed womanhood in your Son who was born of woman. We thank you for the rich heritage that has been granted to this world through its mothers. We children rise up today to call them blessed. As they first taught us of you and often prayed with us and for us, so we pray, lay your hand in tender benediction upon them. Grant us hearts to love them as we ought, and sympathy and understanding to give our love its full expression. Amen.
Adapted from Donald W. Conrad

Thanksgiving Day

Almighty God, creator and preserver of all mankind, our loving heavenly Father, we are reminded on this day, officially proclaimed as a day of thanks, that every good and every perfect gift comes from your hand. You have bestowed loving care on all your creatures. For this we give you thanks, and we praise your name for health, food, and shelter; for an abundance of the necessities of life. You have opened your hand of blessing wide to us who are unworthy of your love. We would pray for more grateful hearts for these things.

We thank you, our Father, for the greatest gift of all, your Son, our Savior and the full salvation provided through him on Calvary; and for the gift of the Holy Spirit, directing us to you, leading us into all truth, and giving us the desire to do such things as are pleasing in your sight. We recognize the danger that these material benefits may overshadow the things of the Spirit. Teach us anew that we do not live by bread alone but by every word which proceeds out of the mouth of God.

Bestow wisdom and patience upon those who have the affairs of state in their keeping, that they may always be open to your will, and with reverence and godly fear, walk in obedience. We desire national prosperity but know that such prosperity is associated with national piety. We need your protecting arms and your comforting blessing each day. May this day be the beginning of a closer walk with you. We ask in Jesus' name. Amen.

Benedictions

The grace of our Lord Jesus Christ be with you all. Amen.

The grace of the Lord Jesus Christ, and the love of God, and the communion of the Holy Spirit be with you all. Amen.

The peace of God, which passes all understanding, keep your hearts and minds in the knowledge and love of God, and of his Son Jesus Christ our Lord; and the blessing of God Almighty, the Father, the Son, and the Holy Spirit, be among you, and remain with you always. Amen.

The Lord bless you and keep you;
the Lord make his face shine upon you
and be gracious to you;
the Lord turn his face toward you
and give you peace.
Numbers 6:24-26

Now I commit you to God and to the word of his grace, which can build you up and give you an inheritance among all those who are sanctified.
Acts 20:32

May the grace of the Lord Jesus Christ, and the love of God, and the fellowship of the Holy Spirit be with you all. Amen.
2 Corinthians 13:14

May the God of peace, who through the blood of the eternal covenant brought back from the dead our Lord Jesus, that great Shepherd of the sheep, equip you with everything good for doing his will, and may he work in us what is pleasing to him, through Jesus Christ, to whom be glory for ever and ever. Amen.
Hebrews 13:20-21

To him who is able to keep you from falling and to present you before his glorious presence without fault and with great joy—to the only God our Savior be glory, majesty, power and authority, through Jesus Christ our Lord, before all ages, now and forevermore! Amen.

Jude 24-25

Additional scriptural benedictions:
Psalm 19:14
Psalm 67:1, 2
Romans 16:27
Ephesians 3:20-21
Ephesians 6:23-24
Philippians 4:7
Philippians 4:23
1 Timothy 1:17
2 Timothy 4:22
Philemon 25
2 Peter 3:18
Revelation 7:12
Revelation 22:21

Poems of Consolation

Death from "Holy Sonnets"

Death, be not proud, though some have called thee
Mighty and dreadful, for thou art not so:
For those whom thou think'st thou dost overthrow
Die not, poor Death; nor yet canst thou kill me.
From rest and sleep, which but thy picture be,
Much pleasure; then from thee much more must flow;
And soonest our best men with thee do go—
Rest of their bones and souls' delivery!
Thou'rt slave to fate, chance, kings, and desperate men,
And dost with poison, war, and sickness dwell;
And poppy or charms can make us sleep as well
And better than thy stroke. Why swell'st thou then?
One short sleep past, we wake eternally,
And Death shall be no more: Death, thou shalt die!
John Donne, 1573-1631

No More Death

No more death; no more sorrow, and no fears;
No valley of the shadow, no more pain!
No weeping, for God dries away the tears,
And dried by him tears never rise again.
*   *   *
No more death! Then take comfort, ye who weep,
Give thanks to God, and raise the bowed head;
They are not lost—'tis "his beloved sleep,"
And he who takes and keeps the holy dead.

Are they not safe with him? And when the veil
Is rent for us, and sight supplanteth faith,
Then, reunited, love shall never fail;
For he hath said, "There shall be no more death."
Henry Drummond, 1851-1897

The Dying Christian to His Soul

Vital spark of heavenly flame!
Quit, O quit this mortal frame!
Trembling, hoping, lingering, flying,
O the pain, the bliss of dying!
Cease, fond Nature, cease thy strife,
And let me languish into life!

Hark! they whisper; angels say:
"Sister Spirit, come away!"
What is this absorbs me quite?
Steals my senses, shuts my sight,
Drowns my spirit, draws my breath?
The world recedes; it disappears!
Heaven opens on my eyes! my ears
With sounds seraphic ring!
Lend, lend your wings! I mount! I fly!
O Grave! where is thy victory?
O Death! where is thy sting?

Alexander Pope, 1688-1744

Crossing the Bar

Sunset and evening star,
    And one clear call for me.
And may there be no moaning of the bar
    When I put out to sea.

But such a tide as moving seems asleep,
    Too full for sound and foam,
When that which drew from out the boundless deep
    Turns again home.

Twilight and evening bell,
    And after that the dark.
And may there be no sadness of farewell
    When I embark.

For though from out our bourne of time and place
    The flood may bear me far,
I hope to see my Pilot face to face,
    When I have crossed the bar.

Alfred Lord Tennyson, 1809-1892

Resignation

There is no death! What seems so is transition.
    This life of mortal breath
Is but a suburb of the life elysian,
    Whose portal we call Death.

She is not dead, the child of our affection,
    But gone unto that school
Where she no longer needs our poor protection,
    And Christ himself doth rule.

       *   *   *

Not as a child shall we again behold her;
    For when with raptures wild
In our embraces we again enfold her,
    She will not be a child;
But a fair maiden, in her Father's mansion,
    Clothed with celestial grace;
And beautiful with all the soul's expansion
    Shall we behold her face.

from Henry Wadsworth Longfellow, 1807-1882

The Eternal Goodness

Within the maddening maze of things,
    And tossed by storm and flood,
To one fixed trust my spirit clings;
    I know that God is good.

I long for household voices gone,
    For vanished smiles I long,
But God hath led my dear ones on,
    And He can do no wrong.

I know not what the future hath
    Of marvel or surprise,
Assured alone that life and death
    His mercy underlies.

And if my heart and flesh are weak
    To bear an untried pain,
The bruised reed He will not break,
    But strengthen and sustain.

And so beside the silent sea
　　I wait the muffled oar;
No harm from Him can come to me
　　On ocean or on shore.

I know not where His islands lift
　　Their fronded palms in air;
I only know I cannot drift
　　Beyond His love and care.
　　　　　　John Greenleaf Whittier, 1807-1892

Well Done

Servant of God, well done!
　　Rest from thy loved employ:
The battle fought, the victory won,
　　Enter thy Master's joy.

The pains of death are past,
　　Labor and sorrow cease,
And Life's long warfare closed at last,
　　Thy soul is found in peace.
　　　　　　James Montgomery, 1771-1854

There is No Death

There is no death! The stars go down
　　To rise upon some other shore,
And bright in Heaven's jeweled crown
　　They shine for evermore.

There is no death! And angel form
　　Walks o'er the earth with silent tread;
He bears our best loved things away,
　　And then we call them "dead."

He leaves our hearts all desolate;
　　He plucks our fairest, sweetest flowers;
Transplanted into bliss, they now
　　Adorn immortal bowers.
　　　　　　from John L. McCreery, 1835-1906

Friends Beyond

I cannot think of them as dead,
  Who walk with me no more;
Along the path of life I tread—
  They have but gone before.

The Father's House is mansioned fair,
  Beyond my vision dim;
All souls are His, and here or there
  Are living unto Him.

And still their silent ministry
  Within my heart hath place,
As when on earth they walked with me,
  And met me face to face.

Their lives are made forever mine;
  What they to me have been
Hath left henceforth its seal and sign
  Engraven deep within.

Mine are thy by an ownership
  Nor time nor death can free;
For God hath given to love to keep
  Its own eternally.
  Frederick L. Hosmer, 1840-1929

Lean on the Lord

Lean on the Lord in thy sorrow;
  Lean on the strength of His arm;
Trust in the word of His promise;
  He will not suffer you harm.
He knows thy troubles aforetime;
  That pave the way for His grace;
He waiteth now for thine asking;
  Why stand aloof from His face?

Lean on the Lord who is waiting above,
Lean on the arm of His infinite love.

Lean on the Lord in thy sorrow;
    Lean on the strength of His might;
Trust in the fullness of mercy;
    He will direct thee aright.
He will not fail in thy trial:
    His are the sources of love;
He is now waiting in heaven,
    Bending with blessing above.

Lean on the Lord who is waiting above,
Lean on the arm of His infinite love.

Clinton Lockhart

Heaven at Last

Angel voices sweetly singing,
Echoes through the blue dome ringing,
News of wondrous gladness bringing;
    Ah, 'tis heaven at last!

On the jasper threshold standing,
Like a pilgrim safely landing;
See, the strange bright scene expanding,
    Ah, 'tis heaven at last!

Sin forever left behind us,
Earthly visions cease to blind us,
Earthly fetters cease to bind us;
    Ah, 'tis heaven at last!

Not a teardrop ever falleth,
Not a pleasure ever palleth,
Song to song forever calleth;
    Ah, 'tis heaven at last!

Christ himself the living splendor,
Christ the sunlight mild and tender;
Praises to the Lamb we render:
    Ah, 'tis heaven at last!

Horatius Bonar, 1808-1889

Hymns of Consolation

Abide With Me

Abide with me: Fast falls the eventide;
The darkness deepens; Lord, with me abide:
When other helpers fail, and comforts flee,
Help of the helpless, O abide with me.

Swift to its close ebbs out life's little day;
Earth's joys grow dim, its glories pass away:
Change and decay in all around I see;
O thou who changest not, abide with me.

I need thy presence every passing hour;
What but thy grace can foil the tempter's power?
Who, like thyself, my guide and stay can be?
Through cloud and sunshine, Lord, abide with me.

I fear no foe, with thee at hand to bless;
Ills have no weight, and tears no bitterness;
Where is death's sting? Where, grave, thy victory?
I triumph still, if thou abide with me.

Hold thou thy cross before my closing eyes;
Shine through the gloom and point me to the skies;
Heaven's morning breaks, and earth's vain shadows flee;
In life, in death, O Lord, abide with me.
Henry Francis Lyte, d. 1847

Children of the Heavenly Father

Children of the heavenly Father
Safely in his bosom gather;
Nestling bird nor star in heaven
Such a refuge e'er was given.

God his own doth tend and nourish,
In his holy courts they flourish;
From all evil things he spares them,
In his mighty arms he bears them.

Neither life nor death shall ever
From the Lord his children sever;
Unto them his grace he showeth,
And their sorrows all he knoweth.

Praise the Lord in joyful numbers!
Your Protector never slumbers;
At the will of your Defender
Every foeman must surrender.

Though he giveth or he taketh,
God his children ne'er forsaketh,
His the loving purpose solely
To preserve them pure and holy.
Carolina Sandel Berg, d. 1903
Tr. Ernst W. Olson, d. 1958

Rock of Ages

Rock of Ages, cleft for me, let me hide myself in thee;
Let the water and the blood, from thy wounded side which
flowed,
    Be of sin the double cure,
    Save from wrath and make me pure.

Not the labors of my hands could fulfill the law's demands;
These for sin could not atone; thou must save, and thou alone:
    In my hand no price I bring;
    Simply to thy cross I cling.

While I draw this fleeting breath, when my eyes shall close in
death,
When I rise to worlds unknown, and behold thee on thy throne:
    Rock of Ages, cleft for me,
    Let me hide myself in thee.
Augustus M. Toplady, d. 1778

Jesus, Lover of my Soul

Jesus, lover of my soul, let me to thy bosom fly,
While the nearer waters roll, while the tempest still is high:
Hide me, O my Savior hide, till the storm of life is past;
Safe into the haven guide; O receive my soul at last.

Other refuge have I none, hangs my helpless soul on thee;
Leave, O leave me not alone, still support and comfort me:
All my trust on thee is stayed, all my help from thee I bring;
Cover my defenseless head with the shadow of thy wing.

Thou, O Christ, art all I want, more than all in thee I find;
Raise the fallen, cheer the faint, heal the sick and lead the blind;
Just and holy is thy name; I am all unrighteousness:
False and full of sin I am; thou are full of truth and grace.

Plenteous grace with thee is found, grace to cover all my sin;
Let the healing streams abound, make and keep me pure within:
Thou of life the fountain art, freely let me take of thee;
Spring thou up within my heart, rise to all eternity.

Charles Wesley, d. 1788

For All the Saints

For all the saints who from their labors rest,
Who thee by faith before the world confessed,
Thy name, O Jesus, be forever blest.
Alleluia, alleluia.

Thou wast their rock, their fortress, and their might;
Thou, Lord, their captain in the well-fought fight;
Thou, in the darkness still, their one true light.
Alleluia, alleluia.

O blest communion, fellowship divine!
We feebly struggle, they in glory shine;
Yet all are one in thee, for all are thine.
Alleluia, alleluia.

And when the strife is fierce, the warfare long,
Steals on the ear the distant triumph song,
And hearts are brave again, and arms are strong.
Alleluia, alleluia.

From earth's wide bounds, from ocean's farthest coast,
Through gates of pearl stream in the countless host,
Singing to Father, Son and Holy Ghost.
Alleluia, alleluia.

William W. How, d. 1897

Death, Where is Thy Sting?

Death, thou hast conquered me:
'Twas by thy darts I'm slain;
But Christ shall conquer thee,
And I shall rise again.

Time hastens on the hour,
The just shall rise and sing;
O grave, where is thy power?
O death, where is thy sting?

Christopher Sauer, Jr., d. 1784

The Strife is O'er

The strife is o'er, the battle done;
The victory of life is won;
The song of triumph has begun. Alleluia!

The powers of death have done their worst,
But Christ their legions has dispersed:
Let shouts of holy joy outburst. Alleluia!

The three sad days have quickly sped;
He rises glorious from the dead:
All glory to our risen Head! Alleluia!

He closed the yawning gates of hell;
The bars from heaven's high portals fell:
Let hymns of praise his triumphs tell. Alleluia!

Lord, by the stripes which wounded thee,
From death's dread sting thy servants free,
That we may live and sing to thee. Alleluia!

From the Latin, c. 1695

Titles of Additional Hymns of Consolation

"All the Way my Savior Leads Me"—*Fanny J. Crosby*
"Face to Face with Christ my Savior"—*Carrie E. Breck*
"Great is Thy Faithfulness"—*Thomas O. Chrisholm*
"It is Well with my Soul"—*Horatio G. Spafford*
"Jerusalem the Golden"—*Bernard of Cluny*
"Lead, Kindly Light"—*John Henry Newman*
"Loved with Everlasting Love"—*George Wade Robinson*
"O God, Our Help in Ages Past:—*Isaac Watts*
"O Love that Wilt Not Let Me Go"—*George Matheson*
"Softly Now the Light of Day"—*George W. Doane*
"Ten Thousand Times Ten Thousand"—*Henry Alford*
"When I Can Read My Title Clear"—*Isaac Watts*

Easter Sunday

(1991-2030)

1991	March	31		2011	April	24
1992	April	19		2012	April	8
1993	April	11		2013	March	31
1994	April	3		2014	April	20
1995	April	16		2015	April	5
1996	April	7		2016	March	27
1997	March	30		2017	April	16
1998	April	12		2018	April	1
1999	April	4		2019	April	21
2000	April	23		2020	April	12
2001	April	15		2021	April	4
2002	March	31		2022	April	17
2003	April	20		2023	April	9
2004	April	11		2024	March	31
2005	March	27		2025	April	20
2006	April	16		2026	April	5
2007	April	8		2027	March	28
2008	March	23		2028	April	16
2009	April	12		2029	April	1
2010	April	4		2030	April	21